Clutterology

GETTING RID OF CLUTTER AND GETTING ORGANIZED!

NANCY MILLER

Published by: CPM Systems

Printed in the United States of America
First Printing, 1999

Publisher's Cataloging-in-Publication
(Provided by Quality Books, Inc.)

Miller, Nancy, 1958-
Clutterology : getting rid of clutter and getting organized! / Nancy Miller. -- 1st ed.
p. cm.
Includes index.
Preassigned LCCN: 97-94722
ISBN: 0-9629944-0-5

1. Storage in the home. 2. Home economics. I. Title.

TX309.M55 1998 648.8
QBI98-1302

Acknowledgments

There are no accidents in life.

To my husband, Mike, whose love, support and encouragement helped to make this book a reality. He is also a source of a lot of love, fun and great stories. We are partners in life and business which is a very rare treat.

To my family—Miriam and Leonard (parents); Rita, Lorna, Dan, Gordy (siblings); aunts, uncles and cousins. Relatively speaking, they are wonderful people and I'm glad I could share them with you, because I think they're very special. I have learned so much from them.

To all the friends who have helped me, thank you for sharing your life's experiences with me. Billie Fergeson, Marguerite Ham, Ed Huser, Andrea Johnson, Dave Morton, Leslie Sears, Anna Tonkin and Jane Zimmerman.

Thanks to Jeri Cohen who provided the 1997 Day-Timer® Survey, and for the services of the cartoonists Bradford Veley and Joe Kohl and to the staff of Lillian Vernon for all their help.

Also, special thanks to Dan Kline for all of his help with the editing and proofing of our books.

Coming Soon in the Clutterology Series

The Clutter Bug Attacks Bedrooms
The Clutter Bug Attacks Children's Rooms
The Clutter Bug Attacks Closets
The Clutter Bug Attacks Collections, Memorabilia and Photographs
The Clutter Bug Attacks Desks
The Clutter Bug Attacks Files
The Clutter Bug Attacks Garages, Attics and Basements
The Clutter Bug Attacks Home Offices
The Clutter Bug Attacks Junk Mail and Telemarketers
The Clutter Bug Attacks Kitchens
The Clutter Bug Attacks Legal Offices
The Clutter Bug Attacks Medical Offices
The Clutter Bug Attacks Offices
The Clutter Bug Attacks Real Estate Office
The Clutter Bug Attacks Sales Offices

Clutter Bug Tips for Bookkeepers and CPAs
Clutter Bug Tips for Dads
Clutter Bug Tips for Moms
Clutter Bug Tips for Newlyweds
Clutter Bug Tips for Real Estate Agents
Clutter Bug Tips for Sales People
Clutter Bug Tips for Secretaries and Assistants
Clutter Bug Tips for Secretary and Boss Teams
Clutter Bug Tips for Seniors
Clutter Bug Tips for Singles
Clutter Bug Tips for Students
Clutter Bug Tips for Teenagers
Clutter Bug Tips for Widow and Widowers
Clutter Bug Tips for Working Mothers

Many of these will be in audiotape and videotape format in addition to the books.

TABLE OF CONENTS

PREFACE

June 1979 I had just completed my second year of college and lined up my summer job. But before the summer became work, my cousin, Andrea (Andy) was getting married and I was her maid of honor.

Andy and her family have always been special to my family and me. Andy is exactly six months older than I am and we had shared many of the same experiences growing up, like 4-H and band. However, Andy was pretty and popular and I wasn't. At 20, I was only beginning to develop a personality.

After the excitement and anxiety of the wedding rehearsal, the wedding party headed for the rehearsal dinner. Since Canby, Minnesota was a very small town, the dinner was held at a restaurant in the larger town of Dawson, about 45 miles away. My cousin, Curt, asked if I would like to ride on his motorcycle. Having been only an occasional passenger, I thought it would be fun.

After the dinner, we headed back to Canby. As dusk approached, Curt slowly maneuvered the bike around the Friday night traffic. As we hit the city limits, Curt accelerated to cruising speed. Within minutes, my attention was drawn to Curt as he began swearing. As my eyes focused forward, I saw headlights coming right towards us. Within seconds, the vehicle had collided with us. The bike spun out of control and we were left lying in the ditch.

Immediately, I ascertained my situation, as my 4-H training had taught me. I could wiggle my toes and fingers so I knew I wasn't paralyzed. In my hands I was holding the bone of my left leg. From afar, Curt yelled, "How are you?"

"I'm fine, but my leg's cut off" I yelled back. Curt went for help. I was conscious and coherent the whole time.

While he was gone, my mind immediately went through denial and bargaining. I had just completed a philosophy course and many other theories went through my mind. In those few moments nothing really changed yet everything had.

Within minutes the first person to come upon the accident was beside me. A strange twist of fate, the first person on the scene was the drunk driver who had hit us and then fled the scene. He had turned back because he saw a police car headed towards him. (In fact, the police car was coming to investigate a deer that had been hit earlier by a car in the area.)

The second vehicle at the scene was my relatives and the wedding party. I will never know the depth of their despair arriving on an accident scene of someone they knew.

An ambulance took me to the local clinic where they stabilized my condition. As the nurse began to prep me, I remembered the care I had taken in choosing my outfit for that evening, mustering every ounce of sexuality that I could create: a white sundress (borrowed), eight rings, two sets of earrings, three necklaces, several bracelets, a watch, two hair combs and contacts. A lot of good they did me now!

Once I was stabilized, I needed to be transferred by ambulance to a larger facility. There were two choices—my hometown of Hutchinson or Willmar. Willmar was where I had gone to community (junior) college. The distance from Dawson to Hutchinson or Willmar was only a matter of a few minutes. I later found out that the closer of the two, Willmar, was chosen based upon the probably of my survival.

My parents met us at the emergency room. An emergency surgical team was assembled. When I awoke after surgery, I was in an intensive care unit. My family was there. I knew immediately that my left leg had been amputated above the knee. I hurt and was in pain. I had no other bruises, scrapes or injuries from the accident other than the amputation.

I had numerous visitors in intensive care. The new bride and groom brought me their wedding bouquet as they headed off to Canada on their honeymoon. An ex-boyfriend had sent a priest; my family sent a minister. Lots of company—I had never been so popular!

Three days later, I was transferred onto the general floor into a private room. The room was needed for the cards, flowers and visitors I was receiving.

I had no restrictions on food and since I had memorized the phone number for pizza delivery, I called and had a pizza delivered to my room. I was the hit of the nursing station when I gave them the leftovers.

Curt, Aunt Emlyn and Uncle Paul came to visit. My ex-boyfriend stopped by, as did college teachers, more relatives and friends. People that I didn't even know stopped by.

While in college, I was involved with Circle K, which is a Kiwanis sponsored collegiate service organization. I was a member of the Minnesota-Dakotas (North and South) Board of Directors at the time.

When I was in the private room, I called my Governor, Lori, to ask if I still had a job. Lori was flabbergasted. She has just been informed about the accident a few hours earlier and here I was on the phone wondering if I still had a volunteer position. Yes, of course, I still had a job!

One of the most touching gestures in my life came from friends in the Circle K Club of Hutchinson when they sent me a dozen roses. A single rose from 12 friends. The Circle K theme that year was Caring Life's Magic. I had never received flowers in my life prior to that point. Here was a beautiful bouquet of long stemmed red roses. And not just from one person, but twelve people! It still brings tears to my eyes.

I was in the hospital a total of six days. Since then, I have become a stronger person but I am the same person today as I was before.

I am not less of a person because a part of my body is gone. I am not handicapped or disabled. I am a woman with one leg, not a one-legged woman. People now notice me and how I look. And I can no longer hide. I am unique and one of a kind!!!

Because of the accident, I became more aware of my surroundings. In some instances, I became an efficiency expert—trying to reduce the time, energy and money that an activity took. One of my priorities was, and still is, safety. I do not like to fall. So I learned to **change the environment** to work for me which became the basis for this book.

As I began getting back to my activities, I attended a Circle K Board Meeting. Somehow (only as college students could do) the question was asked, "what drawer do you put your underwear in?" I thought that everyone was just like me—the upper right drawer. Nooo!!! The replies were top, bottom, left and right. Something so simple (or so I thought) had so many answers. This was my first awareness that people do things differently—even the basics.

Although getting organized will help you, it is not a life or death situation. Sometimes it will feel like it is. Getting organized has helped numerous people cope with life more easily. Have some fun! Try different ideas, different **toys**, and if they work for you, use them. However, the possibility exists that the first time you pick up an organizing toy, it might not be successful for you. Try, try again.

For years, my hobby and interest has been the British Royal Family (the Queen, Diana, Charles, Sarah, Andrew, etc.). I have tried to use examples from their lifestyles to provide a contrast and to add some fun!

Clutterology

GETTING RID OF CLUTTER AND GETTING ORGANIZED!

CHAPTER 1

The Test!

When you are deciding whether to keep, to store or to toss something, ask these questions. The answers change, so don't expect to just ask the question once and get it right. Things that in high school or college days were very important may no longer have the usefulness they once had.

- How do I use this?
- How often do I need this?
- Is this helping me now?
- How much would it cost to replace (money, time or energy)?
- Is this what *somebody* told me? Was this the way I was taught?
- What is the worst thing that could happen? Are you willing to accept those consequences?
- Why do I want/need this?
- Can I obtain it elsewhere?
- How will I use this?
- Is it timely? Is it accurate and reliable?
- How long do I need it?

It All Started When I Was Very Young

Welcome to the wonderful world of order, control and never misplacing a thing—well, perhaps in another world. Most likely, this will not be an ongoing occurrence in your life. There can be periods of happiness.

What is Clutterology? It is the science and study of clutter. All science begins with questions so that is where we will start, with questions. There will be a number of questions for you to ask and answer.

When we take a look at our home life, our work life, and even leisure activities, there seems to be an abundance of clutter in our life. Most of us would like to get rid of the clutter, but don't know how to start.

This book is designed for both the home and office. There are some great ideas that work in the home, and work just as well in the office. Or an idea that works great in the office might spark a solution for the home.

Some people say it's easier to get organized and stay organized at work. At work, systems are designed, established, and in place. Not being organized could result in getting fired, so there is motivation for being organized at work. However, with each passing day, we get more papers and have to do more work with less time spent at home, it's not easy.

Others say that it is easier to get organized and stay organized at home. There are fewer papers, less people and less time. Unlike work, however, you can't quite or fire your family!

It is tough to balance life. However, without understanding the basics, whether you are organized at work or home, it may be just serendipity.

When you were in school (elementary, high school, or college), how many classes did you take for organizing? Five, three or perhaps one. WHAT? None! Perhaps the closest class to getting organized was a home economics class, a business class (filing), or perhaps a psychology class. Even now, we can take a night class on how to collect antique jewelry, etc., but no one addresses how to get rid of it when we're done with it.

It is hard to believe that something so important (and so basic) has been left to nature—not formal education. Perhaps you learned from your parents. Few of us were ever taught how to reduce clutter, but most of us were expected to be organized.

If we were to walk into a hospital that was messy and dirty we might walk out because a hospital is supposed to be clean and germ free.

In the work world, promotions can be influenced by whether or not a person is organized; we tend to get promoted if it looks like we can deal with more responsibilities.

New Year's Resolutions:
Weight loss
Eat healthy
Spend more time with family
Save money
Get organized

Survey by 3M

Have you ever noticed when visiting new home showrooms that the decorator will decorate with a minimum number of items? Or that on television, movies or soap operas no one ever has a pile of papers on their desk.

We have more confidence in orderliness—whether that be a medical doctor's white coat, a CEO's executive office which is spotless, or the President of the United States not carrying his own bags and briefcase. Disorganization is **tolerated** in genius, successful people or creative individuals. You and I are stuck somewhere between the make-believe of Hollywood and genius.

There are three types of individuals that attend seminars, classes or read books about organizational skills.

1. Those that already do it well and are looking to pick up a couple more tips about how to write their own book, give a seminar or become a professional organizer.

2. Those that are interested in **cleaning** up their lifestyle and are taking the first step.

3. Those that know somebody that should attend the seminar or read the books on how to get organized, because **they** need it!

Getting organized is a personal experience. What will work for some, won't work for another (usually the individuals you live with or work with). Throughout this book I have tried to give suggestions, ask questions to spark your imagination, and present both the positive and negative to a suggestion so that you can come up with your own ideas.

Organized and Neat—What's The Difference?

Order is a neat desk, straight rows of razor-sharp pencils, and precisely aligned stacks of paper. Orderliness is next to Godliness. Neat is orderly, groomed, clean, taut, ordered, and prim. Your spouse (boss) should be able to organize you.

Our next door neighbor cleans out the inside of the car muffler (as far as her fingers will go). She will pick up the grate over the drainage hole to remove the leaves and sticks that are there. She is very, very neat (obsessive compulsive).

Being organized requires an inflexible regimen. To be sloppy and disorganized is to be creative, so say the poets of the coffee mug world! Organized is arranged, planned, established, standardized and/or systematized.

There is a difference between being neat and being organized. My husband, Mike, is neat and I am organized. When he wants to clean up his office, he stuffs his stuff into the drawers and closets. When entering my office, you'll have to walk over piles on the floor but if you open the drawers, all the files are labeled and are in alphabetical order. The rules in our offices are—I don't go into his drawers and if he doesn't like my piles, he can close the door.

Here is my definition of organized: if the house or office is organized, it will function while you are not there.

Cliches

For centuries, there have been cliches circulating. Some of the information is truthful, and some of the information is incorrect. How many of the following have you heard?

Everything in its Place! As soon as possible, create a home for the stuff—on the desktop, for example, next to the phone, the lamp, and the stapler, the pen and paper. Immediately you'll see if something is missing or if it has run away from home.

I found this rule hard to follow at times, especially when I was young or just new in a location (job, house, or environment). This is akin to developing a habit. By keeping specific items in their same place, it is easy to find them and easy to put them back. However, I like to keep re-arranging things. The last time that we moved, I promised Mike that I would not move the furniture while he was gone. I could just imagine him walking into a dark house late at night and running right into the furniture!

Use It or Lose It! Although I don't always subscribe to this philosophy, sometimes it does articulate the basic concept for reducing clutter. If it has been a normal year, one year would be a good rule.

> ***"You can never be too rich or too thin"***
> ***The Duchess of Windsor***
>
> ***"... or have too little stuff."***
> ***Nancy Miller***

There does come a point when it is possible to cut back too much. But how far is that? Most of us have enough clothes and food in the house to last a couple of years! Enough paper clips for a couple of life times.

I have an arrangement with Mike to tell me when I have gone too far. **The road to ruin is paved with good intentions.** What was designed to work, then isn't working now.

Do you have a trusted friend that can tell you that you have gone from good intentions to the other side (approaching a cheapskate or scrooge)? If not, develop checkpoints to test yourself, keeping a balance in life.

Pareto Principle or 80/20 Rule! Named after Vilfredo Pareto, a nineteenth-century Italian economist, this principle states that 80 percent of the value of a group of items is generally concentrated in only 20 percent of the items.

The 80/20 rule applies to reducing clutter. When starting out, 80 percent is clutter. As you start to reduce the clutter, the numbers shift to using 80 percent of what you have. No matter how lean and trim you get, there will always be items around that no longer serve their purpose.

The less you have, the more you use it. Haven't you noticed that when you go on vacation and pack two bags of clothes that you use most of them? It seems; however, that there is always something that isn't used. I also know many people that pack **way too much** when they go on vacation—everything that they could possibly ever need.

What You Own, Owns You! On the last day of our honeymoon in Hong Kong, we walked past a furrier. Just for the fun of it, we walked in to look at fur coats. We walked out owning a fur jacket.

This was a gift from my husband; it was a memory from my only trip to Hong Kong. The price of a custom-made jacket was far less than in the States and the design of the jacket was unique. A wise decision—except what you own, owns you.

Never having had a fur coat before, I found that it was not as simple as hanging it in the closet. After wearing it for a couple of events, the clasps didn't stay shut so I had to find someone to work on the fur—not an easy task. Then I found out that I could not hang it in the closet to store it, it had to be stored in cold storage.

A cold storage facility was not in our neighborhood, it was not free and they eventually went out of business. If I wanted to wear the coat, we would have to go down and pick it up (after making arrangements for them to get it from their off-site location). Then I had to take it back. Then there was the added insurance. Then there was the uncomfortable situation in the States that there are many people that do not like real furs on people and who are very vocal.

I would have been much happier without it—but the darn thing won't wear out.

Our things can't take care of themselves. We have to take care of them! If you are looking to save time, reduce the number of things that you have to take care of. A one-room house takes less care than a 10,000 square foot house. If there are other things in life that you would rather do than clean, a smaller house might help.

Creating The Basics

Reduce first to get organized! The logic of this is, if you have several hundreds of books, and you organize them first, it is possible to spend several hundreds of dollars buying bookshelves. Then, when the bookshelves have been installed and the books are put on the shelf, you realize that you don't like any of those books or are never going to read them. The money to purchase the shelves was wasted.

> ***Clutter is anything that is excess for you.***

If you feel that you want to keep what you have, continue on to another suggestion. However, if you continue to do the same thing, don't expect the results to change! That means that if you want to have a life that is organized, **indiscriminate** collecting of everything won't achieve organization.

There are three stages for objects or information. They are past, present and future. We are all familiar with thinking about time in the past, present and future, so we are taking something familiar and giving it a new twist.

Past

These are things that were once useful, but their **usefulness to you** has gone. Often times, just tossing them out will do. For some, tossing is cruel and unnecessary. Create a new home for the items that you no longer need, whether that is a family member, a friend or a charity.

There are a number of charities that are pleased to receive your donations. This is also an area where you can be a little creative. Do you have a favorite charity or cause?

Food banks operate 365 days a year—not just at Christmas time. In cleaning out your cupboards, is there unopened food that could be donated to a food bank in June? (See page 35) When I see individuals on the streets with signs that say *Will Work for Food!* I am tempted to just give them the bag of food from the cupboard.

> ***35% of Americans give to charity at least once a month***
>
> ***from Statistics about Americans***

The United States Postal Service (USPS) especially the National Association of Letter Carriers has a wonderful program in conjunction with Campbell Soups. Two Saturdays in May the letter carries will pick up food while on their regular route. There are local coordinators who work with local food banks and all you have to do is leave the food out.

Look in the telephone book for the local branch of Goodwill or Red Cross. Phone books dedicate the first few pages to the charitable organizations in the community.

Each of the local Salvation Army Corps reflects the needs of that community. Contact the local Corps and ask about their needs. If the area has an Adult Rehabilitation Center and operates a thrift store, they usually have a central location or will pick up items. Donated items may be tax deductible.

Contact the **hospitals**. For years, Mike and I have asked our friends who remember our birthdays to give us unwrapped children's toys that we send to Children's Hospitals.

The local **libraries** often look for books and magazines, which they sell to help buy new books. (See page 126 for further guidelines and suggestions.)

With cut backs in budgets, **schools** are in need of items as simple as pens and pencils. Contact the English department or perhaps the drama department for donating items (won't it be a hoot to go to a high school production and see your *old* clothes on stage?)

Women's **shelters** have different names in different cities. Because of the nature of the work (family violence), the address or perhaps even the phone numbers aren't listed. Talk to the police, fire department or ministers as they may be able to coordinate your donations.

Consignment Stores are another place to take items and make a little money at the same time. Call the store first. Find out what type of items they want. There are stores for children items, sports equipment, men's clothing, women's clothing and even evening wear. If your items don't sell, donate them to charity.

Consignment stores for kid's clothes and toys are terrific. Kids seem to grow daily and get bored with their toys on the days they're not growing. Contact a local store near you.

Charity Box. An idea from another organizer was to have a permanent container for charity. Whenever you have an article of clothing, a jigsaw puzzle or a pen and pencil set that you want to donate, it goes into the container. (See page 6 for Everything In Its Place.)

Line the container with a heavy-duty trash liner. When the container is full, simply lift out the liner and take it to the charity drop-off. One of my students in a seminar mentioned that she keeps a clipboard with the box and as things are put into the box, she makes a notation of what the item is, the quantity and the value. This is her record for a tax donation.

This is a nice *staging* area. If you have something that you don't know if you need, you can put it in this container. In the next 30 days if you find that you need it, you can always retrieve it. For years we used a public storage facility. When we were no longer using something, we took it down to storage. After a few years, we were ready for it to find a new home, or donated to a charity. (See page 98.)

If you find that you are retrieving everything that you put in this container, make plans to take it to the charity *daily* so your are not constantly retrieving it.

Future

The only reason to file or store an item is if you will want or need to use it again in the future.

> According to a recent survey of the American Business Women's Association, 43 percent of respondents waste 15 minutes every day looking for lost items. Another 32 percent waste up to 30 minutes a day.

Before storing items away, consider long-term, what might happen? It is not an uncommon story when someone has stored paperwork, then retrieved it, to find the items were destroyed or ruined by the elements. Is the chosen location free from moisture? Bugs? Mildew? If there is moisture, consider using plastic boxes or lining paper boxes with trash can bags. Are the items affected by heat? Find another location rather than the attic for this item.

When storing items, be sure to label the box. Label each side as well as the top and the bottom (if you could see it). Ask whose, what, where, when, how and put that information on the label.

Label the spine of the three ring notebooks that are on the bookshelf or in the file drawers. The idea is that if you were not around, someone else would be able to find what they are looking for. (See page 6.)

Whose stuff is this anyway? Is it yours? A partner's? A child's?

What is this stuff? Describe the items so that the items could be quickly identified. Describe the items so that someone else could identify them. List the contents.

Where did this stuff come from? This answer needs a little creativity. Did you get it as a gift from somebody—Aunt Edith? Are these Christmas decorations for the front porch? Did you buy it on vacation—1991 trip to London, England?

When did you put items in the box? Date the box with the month and year (01/99). This serves as a general indicator in relation to the date that you find the box again. What? 10 years ago!

Labeling boxes also works great for office supplies. Have you ever wondered how long a box of paper clips lasts? Date the side of the box when you order it. When it comes time to re-order, just check the side of the box. If it has been a short period of time (whatever that means to you, your office, your budget and the difficulty in re-ordering) expand the order. Or, if it has been a long period of time, consider reducing the quantity ordered. All items have a shelf-life.

How long should you keep it? If you're using storage boxes as a staging area (keeping an item for a short time, seeing if you missed it and then tossing it out) indicate the date to destroy the contents or how to get rid of them (charity, friends, etc.).

How much stuff do you have in the box—2 dozen candlesticks? Or how much did it cost? $1, $10, or $100?

Emilie Barnes, in *The 15-Minute Organizer*, designed another system of storing boxes. Instead of labeling the boxes with the contents, the box is simply numbered. This way the boxes can be re-used. Before going to storage she knows what box to select (instead of rummaging through all of them) and if a burglar stops by your house, numbers don't mean a whole lot. The contents of the box are listed on index cards and filed in the house.

Present

Newsflash:

you aren't going to change!!

How many of us have tried to change our spouse when we got married? Real successful wasn't it?

There are some things that do change or can be altered, but for the most part, you have habits and styles that aren't going to change. So why try? Instead, **change your environment**.

It is much easier to put a hamper where your spouse drops the clothes rather than nag your spouse forever to put the clothes in the hamper. Once these little tricks are taught, then perhaps you can add another trick (move the hamper to the side of the room instead of the middle).

Does this sound like training an animal? Am I comparing our spouses to training an animal? Well no ... well yes. In high school, I was involved in dog training. One statement the instructor made (and when I became an instructor, I used) was that the handler only has two seconds to correct a dog after a mistake. Why? Because in three seconds, the dog has forgotten what it did and is thinking about something else.

My husband has asked that I catch him in the act, rather than waiting until two or three days later to tell him about it. Great idea. Three days later, he can't go back and undo it. Only when it's happening can we change.

When I was learning to downhill ski, my instructor told me that the first time I fell getting off the chair lift, it was an accident. The second time I fell getting off the chair lift, it was a coincidence. The third time, it was a habit.

Unconscious habits seem to pop up over night (or only after three times). However, experts say that to consciously create a habit takes 21 consecutive days. I haven't been that consistent in my life, so, I change my environment.

Place Things Where You Use Them. How often are you looking for something and it never seems to be at hand? You have to get it out, and then put it back. Wouldn't it be simpler if you just had it there in the first place? Great clues for this type of situation is to look where stuff is dropped or left. Do the kids drop their clothes at the front door? Put a coat rack there. Do you take off your clothes in the bedroom or in the bathroom? If it is the bedroom, why is the clothes hamper in the bathroom?

As in real estate, a business location that is easily accessible and convenient has a higher rent than the upper floor of a building in the back by the alley. Let's apply that logic to our space.

Stand in the middle of the kitchen (bathroom, office, etc.) and reach out your arms. What you can touch is the prime real estate. Put things in these locations that you need **daily**.

Take a step forwards, backwards, sideways, bend and stretch. This is secondary space. This is where things that are used on a weekly basis are placed.

The third area is climbing and crawling space. These are areas that are the most difficult to get to. This is where things that are used infrequently are placed.

Make your systems easy to use. An important *Clutter Bug* rule is **simplify**. We are forever trying to complicate things.

> ***"Life is frittered away by detail. Simplify. Simplify."***
>
> ***Henry David Thoreau***

It is ironic that we are a society that craves organization and orderliness, but does not respect simplicity. Even the English language is difficult rather than simplistic. How many different meanings are there for the word cool (temperature and an expression of acceptance)? How often are manuals written that are pages and pages and pages long, when only a page or two would have worked?

As an engineer, my husband was working on an electronic board. A friend of his walked by and said, "You've used too many parts, reduce it." Mike immediately got defensive and said, "You have no idea what I'm working on! How do you know that there are too many parts?" The friend replied, only as a friend could, "Because I know you, and you have too many parts." A week later when the friend walked by again, he noticed that the board had significantly fewer parts.

Tools of the Trade

Create new uses for containers. Just because something was designed to hold food or trash doesn't mean that it couldn't be used for clothes, paper clips, or a hundred other things. Think of different ways to use stuff.

Use a 55-gallon trash container for a hamper—it's big and everything fits inside on a weekly/bi-weekly basis and the wheels are wonderful.

Zip lock sandwich bags work wonderfully for many types of things—but rarely sandwiches. I like quart size freezer bags, which are larger and more durable. These bags are:

- Multiple sizes.
- Easy to close.
- Not bulky—they don't take much space.
- See-through.
- Re-usable.
- Leak-proof/air tight (to a point).

There are very small bags (the type you would get at a jewelry store). Talk to a jeweler and they might give or sell you a few small bags.

Xpedx Paper Store
106 S Santa Fe Dr
Denver CO 80223
303-777-6688

Consolidated Plastic Co, Inc.
8181 Darrow Rd
Twinsburg OH 44087
800-362-1000

Ask for their catalog. They have a variety of sizes and shapes. However, the order is by the case rather than individual lots.

Tupperware or Rubbermaid products are great all over the house. The sandwich size containers are wonderful for pens, pencils, paper clips, makeup, or nuts and bolts. Because I am not the cook of the house (in fact, we eat out frequently) most of our Tupperware is in every room but the kitchen! Shop on-line at www.rubbermaid.com

Two other products that are very helpful: a **dishpan** and a **kitty litter pan**. These products can be used for everything—to keep craft projects in, as an in-box, or for storing legal size documents. They are a great size and they don't break.

True Cost or Price

It is not just the purchase price of an object that should be considered, but also the cost to replace it, the cost to store it and the energy cost to maintain it.

Cost of Replacement. Can you afford to replace it? While I was in college, the answer was no. I turned shampoo bottles on end getting the very last drop out. If my billable time is $250 an hour as a consultant or $12 per hour when I worked for a temporary agency and I use one minute (or 20¢) of my time. Is it worth the pennies I save?

Antiques and heirlooms, which have sentimental value, would not fall into this category. (See page 159 and 130 for ideas.)

Cost of Storage. What is the cost to store this piece? Take the total rent or mortgage, divide by the square foot, multiply it by the number of years that you are keeping it (or plan to keep it). If the storage cost is $20 for a pencil that you are **not** using and it costs 14¢, what do you think?

If you were to rent a storage space, which is 5 feet deep, 7 feet wide and 8 feet high, it would cost approximately $69 per month. A large unit (10x10) is $82-$95 per month (if a unit is available). A small unit (5x5) is $30-45 per month.

Cost of Energy. One of the under utilized equations is energy cost. How much of your energy will it take to clean, store, move, think about or worry about the purchase? A new car is grand, but if you constantly worry that it will get dented, dinged, etc. perhaps an old car would not have as high of a cost.

"We're not talking about rocket science here!"

Mary Lou "Bunky" Lundberg
Professional Organizer
Chaos Cancelled
Denver Colorado

Mike and I worked out at a gym for years. We decided to go out and buy some home equipment. Even though we had the **habit** of exercising, it was more of a **social** reward to get out of the house. We moved that equipment from room to room trying to find the place where we would use it. We never did find that magical place! Even changing the environment didn't work in this case.

Exercise equipment that is not used but that is cleaned around or used as a clothes rack has a high energy cost. Also, there is the guilt factor. Every time we see the exercise equipment but don't exercise, there is a small voice inside us that says; "You should be doing those exercises!"

Craft projects or baking/cooking equipment could also fall into this category. Are you saying to yourself, "But I should be baking for the kids!" These all have a high energy cost.

Garage Sale

Some people love garage sales. It is a way to make money or to find some great goodies.

Before undertaking a garage sale, consider the total cost of the garage sale: the cost of your time to price the items, the cost to operate the garage sale, the cost to advertise, and the cost of the aggravation. Is it worth your time and effort? Would it be simpler to make donations to charity? If you are still interested in garage sales, check this book out.

Backyard Money Machine: How to Organize and Operate a Successful Garage Sale
by Les R. Schmeltz
Price: $9.95 Paperback 224 pages
ISBN: 0963532103
Practical advise, checklist, sample promotional pieces, displays, crime prevention and clean-

> **It is estimated that $2 billion is spent at garage sales.**
>
> **- Les Schmeltz**

Setting and Determining Limits

The one thing that we have to do (and we really, really hate to do) is set limits for ourselves. What does this mean? It means, select a number and that's the limit.

What is your closet space, your office space, or what is your environment limiting you too? If your closet is only 2x2, it is not possible to put more than that amount in the closet, no matter how organized you get. You now have a choice. Do you remodel the closet or do you get rid of what you can't fit into the closet?

How often do you wash clothes, go grocery shopping or order supplies? Once a week. Fine!!! Great!!! Now the limit of clothes/food/supplies is a week's worth. Know **your** habit.

But, you have no idea what to limit yourself to (how much you need)? Pick a number from thin air. This is like creating a budget for the first time. If, in the past you haven't recorded the numbers, just pick a number. Then, review it on a regular basis to see if this works for you.

The "I Might Need It Someday" Exercise

This is a very interesting and revealing exercise. The directions are very easy. Ask these three questions. The answers are very insightful. If you are having a problem deciding whether or not to keep something, do this exercise.

First Question: **Why** do I need this?

First Answer: Because I might need it someday.

That is a very good answer. Congratulations. We have all been taught that answer. Continue based on the first answer.

Second Question: **Why** might I need it someday? The answer becomes a little more difficult. What would that *need someday* look like (put parameters on it—who, what, where, when, how works well).

Second Answer: Well, because if I am ever in an earthquake this could come in handy!

This is a very good and logical answer. Congratulations. Now, let's go to the third question.

Third Question: **Why** might I be in an earthquake ... do I not have a safety (survival) kit or an emergency plan?

Third Answer: Well, yes, I have all the emergency supplies located ... and the emergency plan is in place.

Then the use of this item is not what it first appeared to be. At first (because I might need it some day) the answer had merit. However, looking more closely at the answer, there was no merit.

Chapter 1—Clutter Bug's Keys to Success

1. To be neat doesn't necessarily mean that we are organized. Neat and organized are two different things.

2. Create homes for items. It is easier to find and put back items.

3. Develop a system for re-cycling unwanted items (giving to charities, friends, selling, etc.).

4. Label everything (except people) so that the next time you try to find it, you can. If the item is not used, you will know how long it has been unused.

5. Having sorted through a project, pile, a desk or a room, and quickly do it a second time. It is amazing how much stuff is still there that you don't need.

Clutterology

GETTING RID OF CLUTTER AND GETTING ORGANIZED!

CHAPTER 2

98B
0320
5137
322
10025
A57
G17
A120
N732

How Come We Can't Eat Out All The Time?

The kitchen can be the conference area, the recreation area, the message area, the staging area, the eating area, the talking area, and the office area—planning for the kitchen is key.

My mom's idea of a perfect kitchen was one where she could stand in the center, stretch out her arms and be able to reach the sink, refrigerator, stove and cupboards without walking more than a step or two. What she ended up with was a farmer's kitchen where she had to walk across the room to get from one appliance to another (before remodeling).

Let's take a look at some of the different parts (and pieces) of the kitchen.

Appliances

Do you have both a manual can opener and an electric can opener in the house? Are you saving the manual unit for a rainy day? Are you waiting for the electric unit to break? How long has it been since the electric unit broke? Has it been over a year? Is it now safe to give the manual unit or the electric unit (the one not being used) to a charity or family member? What is the worst that could happen? Are you willing to accept those consequences?

In today's world, most items purchased five years ago are now technologically obsolete. The item might still work however; the replacement is better, cheaper, does more and is probably smaller. So why are you keeping the parts of a toaster that is 20 years old? If you use the equation of the cost of storage (not including the cost of energy each time you moved or touched the piece) the true cost is hundreds of times more than a replacement part or a new unit. (See page 17.)

How much will it cost to fix it? My husband's business is marketing. He isn't an expert on fixing appliances and he doesn't like to fix things. Taking it to someone that can fix it quickly and without hassle is easier than having it on his eternal *to do* list. (See page 161.)

Do you have all the parts and pieces to use the appliance? This past year, these words came back to haunt us. We both thought that we had something which we didn't—a chaffing dish (but we had the sterno cans). We still aren't sure what happened to it!

Do you have appliances that you received when you got married and have never used? Bun warmers, hot trays or hot plates or even electric frying pans? What about that waffle maker that has been replaced by frozen waffles that pop into the toaster? Don't shuffle (trying to find a new home for it)—re-cycle.

Baskets

Do you have bread baskets (or baskets in general), or trivets in the kitchen drawer? Instead, put the baskets or trivets on the wall as decorations. Then when you need it, simply take it off the wall. When done with the meal, hang it back up.

In one of my homes, I put baskets in stairways. It was a nice way to decorate the space. My sister has baskets along the top edge of her kitchen cabinets. When decorating with baskets, especially if you plan to use them while entertaining, how easily accessible are they? We frequently like to hang the baskets high. To get them down or to hang them up, all we have to do is take one of my crutches and pop it off or on!

Wicker and basket materials can snag. Perhaps line the basket with plastic or a decorative cloth napkin, towel and handkerchief to prevent snags.

Coffee Cups and Mugs

This is getting down to the simple. But nothing is too simple to take a cold hard look at. Mugs seem to be a collection that just happens. They seem to multiply overnight!

Let's start with reduce. What mugs don't work? Is it chipped? If it is (and there is no sentimental attachment) toss it. If there is sentimental attachment, fix the mug. If it is not possible to fix the mug, put it in a place of honor where you can stir those sentimental feelings. Use the mug to hold makeup or use it as a planter!

Does it dribble when you drink from it? Does it tip over easily? If the answer is yes to any of these, toss it out. Do you like coffee cups or mugs? Mugs, then re-cycle the cups.

How many do you need? Don't know? Then how many do you use? Break it down a little more—how many do you use in a week? That's how many mugs?

What is the maximum number of people that you have over on a regular basis? How about for Easter, Christmas, Thanksgiving? Could you use paper cups instead? (See page 31 for big sized events.)

Did your dishes come with cups and saucers? How many? Could you use these instead of the collection of mugs? What is the worst thing that could happen? When company comes, there won't be enough matching sets? Do you even use saucers anymore?

What does it cost? Can you afford to replace them? If so donate the mugs to charity.

Warning: the cute little phrases on the side of the cups do affect us. I have always believed that even the most innocent comment can have a profound impact. Do you want your children growing up and reading everyday "Somedays I wake up grumpy, other days, I just let him sleep"? Get rid of the negative (not politically correct) mugs.

Command Central

Create a central location to coordinate activities, messages and lives. The kitchen has long been a family favorite, but it is by no means the only location, some possible places are (where ever you meet together):

- A bathroom (or just outside the bathroom door).
- The garage.
- The hallway.
- The entryway.
- The parent(s) room (or just outside the door).
- Near the TV/computer.

In this central location keep items such as receipts for shoe repairs, dry cleaners, TV repair store, vacuum repair store, etc. Establish a family activity calendar, which includes scheduled appointment (yours and theirs), school projects, deadlines, and sports schedules. (See page 114 for additional calendaring suggestions.)

Cookbooks and Recipes

My husband collected cookbooks and I could not understand it at all. How many cookbooks does a person need? Get one and that's it. Well, not for him. He actually enjoys reading a cookbook (something I had never heard of before or enjoyed myself). We had put the cookbooks in the kitchen, but I found that I was constantly dragging the cookbooks back after he would take them out to read. So, I just put all the cookbooks in the location where he most commonly reads them. **Change your environment**. (See page 14.)

There are software cookbooks. I like this software because if I only have a bag of coconut flakes in my cupboard, I can search for recipes that have the ingredient of coconut flakes.

Are you a constant clipper of recipes? How do you go about organizing recipes? This is a two-step process: those recipes that have been just clipped and those recipes that you have used.

Sort the clipped recipes (untried) into general categories—desserts, breads, soups, etc. and put them in sheet protectors (the kind that you pick up at the stationery store). Test (try) the recipe and see if you like it. Although it doesn't happen that often, sometimes the recipes can be printed incorrectly. If you do like it, put it with your *keeper recipes* (tried and true).

Now set a limit. How many recipes are needed? How many recipes for banana bread do you need? 1 or 2 perhaps but 8 or 10, probably not (unless you are a cook who specializes in banana bread).

44% reuse tinfoil

from Statistics about Americans

When adding the new recipe, take a moment to toss out the recipe that this will **replace**. Toss one that is too high in cholesterol, takes too long to make, or uses ingredients that you don't normally have around.

I came across this neat recipe indexer. The Recipe Index ($12.95) is for cookbook collectors and the book is designed to help you find the recipe you want when you want it. Also, Maria has Recipes from *Our Family Tree* ($13.95). Great for family reunions, shows gifts, wedding, etc.

Maria Baker The Kitchen Collection
9 Narvaez Way
Hot Springs Village AR 71909
501-922-4373

Century Photo Products and Accessories
PO Box 2393
Brea CA 92822
800-767-0777 www.20thcenturydirect.com
Century Photo has a recipe album with an easel-back design, three ring plastic sheets, which protect the recipes. Many of their products are archival safe.

Coupons

When using coupons keep in mind that the cost of your time and energy should be included. Often people buy products that they would never buy just because there is a coupon. Use determines needs.

My mother-in-law loved her coupons. Whenever a new food came out and the coupon came in the mail, she would purchase it. When she died, her cupboards were full of food that she never used–and didn't even like. Where are you when you need the coupon? We store our coupons in the glove compartment of the car, that way they are with us when we need them.

There are a number of sites on the Internet that offer coupons just for visiting the site. Check them out:

H.O.T. Coupons www.hotcoupons.com
Coupons On-line www.couponsonline.com
Quick Coupons www.qponz.com
Coupon1 www.coupon1.com
Coupon Network www.coolsavings.com

Cupboards

When organizing the kitchen, first think of how you (and your family) are going to use the kitchen and for what purpose. Don't let what *they* designed it for force conformation.

Think of the cupboard space this way using the chart below. Anything with a **+** is good. Locations with a **-** are less desirable and are good for items that are not used on regular basis or items that are large and can be easily seen.

middle front	++	used everyday
middle back	+-	used weekly
high front	-+	used monthly
low front	-+	used monthly
high back	--	used annually
low back	--	used annually

Storage spaces that are high, but easily seen, are good places to store things, but only put things one deep (or two deep if they are identical). Just because you have the space, doesn't mean that it **has** to be used. (See page 171.)

I clean up the kitchen (some of the time) and unload the dishwasher (most of the time) while Mike is fixing the meal. Right next to the dishwasher is the cupboard that is designed for dry goods. For us, this is where the dishes are stored. I need to be able to stay out of Mike's way when he is cooking (and when I come into the kitchen, I do ask for permission).

For me, with the crutches, I don't bend over very easily, so the space nearest the floor is usually left unused. Or I use a kitty litter pan (see page 16), which I can pull out, and everything is right there (pot lids, towels, etc.). Because both Mike and I are tall, higher is more favorable than lower. Perhaps in your home, lower is more favorable than higher. What ever you like to do is how you should adapt your environment.

We like to have our counters clear (not clean but clear). We do not have toasters, crocks full of spoons, floor/sugar/tea canisters sitting on top of the counter. Stuff on the counter tops look good to start with, but picks up grease and dirt over the years. Look at magazines, new model homes or television shows. They don't have stuff on counter tops (except perhaps for Martha Stewart's!).

For years, we had our cutting knives in the drawer (Lillian Vernon—see page 47). Recently Mike commented that it was not convenient for him to get a knife out of the drawer when he needed it (the cutting board was above a knife drawer), so we purchased a knife block and their home (see page 6) is now on the counter. Yes, do have something out on the counter if it works for you. Use determines location.

If you have children, consider placing their dishes or dishes for setting the table at their height. Make it easy for the children. Don't stack items more than two or three high (even for adults).

Dishes

When Mike and I got married, we each had a household that we brought together. For years we had more glasses and mugs than we used. 99 wineglasses and 30 mugs. (See page 151 for additional suggestions.)

We found a great use for the wineglasses. Whenever someone was getting married or had an anniversary, they would get a basket with cheese, crackers, wine and two wineglasses. The mugs were used to put jellybeans in and used as gifts.

Just recently, we purchased a set of wineglasses. Before I purchased the glasses, I asked several ladies in my woman's club that were married in the 60's and 70's what they would recommend if they had to do it over again when it came to stemware. One lady said that she would have liked *one size* because there was always one size that broke and then there wasn't a correct set. So we chose a size that works for white wine, red wine, water, whatever. Keep it simple.

Are there special serving dishes that you are saving just for entertaining? Why? When was the last time you entertained? Last week? Great. Did you use those special-serving dishes or did you grab the closest thing at hand (the everyday dishes)?

We have parties for up to 100 peoples on a yearly basis and we don't have a whole lot of special serving dishes. What we found is we use what we have. We have come up with some very creative ways of serving foods. Remember the saying about the mother of necessity? We put bread sticks in a vase. We have used wine decanters for serving soda pop. It feels so elegant to have our beverage poured out of a decanter. Won't the kids be thrilled to have their milk poured out of the wine decanter?

How many ashtrays do you have around, just waiting for that day or two when you have company over that smokes? It isn't necessary to keep ashtrays around, unless you smoke.

We use our china hutch to store and display our silver and crystal. We attached a timer to the plug so that the hutch would be lit for a couple of hours. This gives you a chance to enjoy it. Great ambiance and a night-light!

What kind of events and activities will you be doing that require special dishes?

Big sized events: are you keeping dishes for those big events (graduation, confirmation, weddings, etc.)? How often do you have them (once every five years)? Is there a rental store in your neighborhood (or in the city) that would rent this stuff?

Medium sized events: Christmas and Thanksgiving come to mind. We have friends and family over but we don't have to overly impress them. Could you use the regular size dishes instead of the super size-serving platter and still make do?

Family events: picnics or BBQ. Are there special dishes? Do you still participate in these activities or these events?

Is there any theme dishes hanging around the house? Sushi or Japanese dishes that you used once or for a short period but aren't using anymore? Don't shuffle—re-cycle.

Most of us grew up hearing, "put that back, those are our good dishes and used when company comes." It is surprising that when company comes, they eat off the everyday dishes, and the good dishes are gathering dust.

My mother is probably typical of many people. She has good dishes and everyday dishes. I remember one year; my sisters purchased a set of dishes for everyday use. Well, mother liked the dishes so much that she keeps them for *everyday company*. This means that she has a set of good china, good everyday stoneware, and everyday dishes. But her preference is to uses paper plates as often as possible!

China products were designed for use. Bone china has small pieces of bone in them, which makes the china very durable even when used everyday. The more silver is used, the less tarnished it looks. (A good place to store your silverware is in a Tupperware container.)

We have three sets of dishes. Our everyday dishes are Corelle®, which don't break; our good china is handed down from our families and we have Christmas china.

The first china pattern that I purchased was a Lenox Christmas pattern. I love Christmas and in college, Christmas was the only time that I had the time or money to entertain. As a young married couple, Christmas was also the only time that we seemed to have more than one couple over. For eight years, that Christmas china was used regularly. We entertained from Halloween to February 1st using our Christmas dishes. People had no idea that we didn't have another set of good china.

Do you have items that you would like to keep but are not in good condition? Look in the Yellow Pages (or the Internet) under antiques repairs and restoring. Frequently they can repair the items. Ozzie's does mail order business also.

Ozzie's Fine Arts
(restoration of furniture, crystal, porcelain, and silver plating)
1701 Artesia Blvd
Manhattan Beach, CA 90266
310-379-2955.

Drawers

Office Tip

The kitchen drawers are a particularly cluttered place because it seems that kitchen gadgets have small pieces, which are stored in the drawer.

Once a year or on a regular basis (quarterly or every six months):

- Take out everything from the drawers and put it on top of the table. Use a tablecloth on the dining room table to protect it's surface.
- Match up parts and pieces. Be sure that everything is there. Are there any pieces missing? (See page 24.)
- Look at the condition of each item. Is it in good working condition? If not, toss or donate.
- Observe the quantity of the items. How many spoons do you have? How many do you need? Which one do you like?
- Put the left over or lost pieces in a plastic bag. Mark the bag with the month/year. If a year from now you haven't found the pieces, toss the bag. If you have found all the pieces, put it together.
- **Fix It**—get out the glue gun, etc. and fix the stuff that needs to be fixed.
- **Store It**—you have three dozen wooden spoons, store the extras in a box. Mark the box (see page 12).

- **Toss It**—is the item beyond repair? This is a good time to get rid of the tools in *not so perfect* working order. If you have a wooden spoon that had a fight with the disposal (and is the one you always seem to grab when you're in a hurry), either replace it because you like the size/feel or get rid of it because you already have a replacement in the drawer.

If you find that the container that you are using to hold the items are slipping around as you open and close the drawer, go to the office supply store. Either get double-faced tape (earthquake squares) or a roll of Velcro® tape. Use the Velcro® if there is any likelihood that you would like to remove the container anytime in the future. It stays in place.

A wonderful trick for cleaning out the drawers is to get a can of compressed air (the type that is used for computers) and spray the drawer. It's easier than a damp cloth or getting the vacuum cleaner. It works best if it is a small project.

Food Storage

Growing up in Minnesota, my mother had a couple of freezers and would purchase a half a side of beef at a time. There was a date set for food shopping (Saturdays) and then Wednesdays would be the day to replenish the perishables (milk and bread).

When I moved away from home, I had a different set of values. I would go to the store on an irregular basis, not the most practical use of time and energy.

When purchasing in bulk, consider:

- Do you like it? If you don't like it in the first place, don't buy it. Some of the club stores have hindered rather than helped people (but I only need 1 not 100!) because up front the bulk price looks like a good deal.

- Just because it costs less in bulk doesn't mean that there is a true savings. Add in the cost of storage and energy.

- Are you likely to use more because you have more? Watch to see that you aren't encouraging wastefulness.

- Do you have the room for it? Many homes nowadays don't have all the extra room for the bulk food.

- Where do you live? How far is the store from you? The further the store, the more storing up that can be done.

We have all purchased something special, which remains in the cupboard (remember my mother-in-law page 28). A clever solution is to clean out the cupboards yearly. Donate the canned dry goods to a food bank or food shelter. (See page 9.)

One of my students knew she would be getting laid off (the grant money was running out). So, as a game for her, she started to cut down on food purchases by using the food that was in the cupboards. She was at two months and counting without any major food purchase. (See page 163.)

Trash Cans

I looked for years to find just the right size trash can that would work for us. I like to throw stuff (I'm not going to change) so the cans had to have a large opening. Mike doesn't like to take out the trash more than once a week, so it has to be big enough for one week's worth of stuff.

I had plastic containers that I used to store collectible magazines. I sold the magazines and had the containers left over. They are only about knee high but are large. We have one for trash and one for re-cycling.

I like to have the containers lined with a plastic trash bag and we drop the whole roll of trash bags in the bottom of the container. As we pull out the trash, the next bag (which is still attached) will be within arms reach and all that needs to be done is to tear the bags apart. If the attached bags are too cumbersome, then detach the bag first.

If there are different sized containers and it is difficult to match up the container with the liner, trying using colored liners. Or perhaps, take a picture of the container and then keep the end-flap of the box matching them together. (See page 104.)

Paper Towels

Does your family go through a lot of paper towels? Why? Before you scream at me "because we need and use them," have you thought about using towels or cloth napkins? That's what they were invented for.

But, you say, cloth napkins are for company. Isn't your family as special as company? But, I would be washing day and night if we did that. Cloth napkins can be used more than once before being washed. There are occasional exceptions. (See page 19.)

But, the napkins are too small. Then use a dishtowel! But a dishtowel is too puny, it doesn't absorb anything. Go down to a discount warehouse store or a paint store. Find the terry cloth towels that absorb everything. We found paint rags or shop towels that work fine, and they have only been used in the kitchen.

Refrigerator

Does your refrigerator look like a war zone with notes and dates? There is a product from Day Runner® that helps to keep the refrigerator looking like a refrigerator.

The Horizontal Home Manager™ Organizer with File Pockets includes a calendar, white board, a pocket for coupons, and a

Hi, John's answering machine is broken. This is his refrigerator. Please speak very slowly, and I'll stick your message to myself with one of these magnets!!!

pocket for pen/pencils. Available locally or call 800-643-9923.

How many magnets do you have? How many do you use? Is one enough? Is there one you don't like? Get rid of that one? Is there one that doesn't stay straight or is always falling off? Get rid of it. Are the magnets just collecting dust?

Tablecloths

Where do you keep your tablecloths? Get rid of those that are too much work, that are soiled, that need to be fixed, or that are too long. Do you need a tablecloth?

Hang tablecloths in the closet or fold and keep them in the linen closet or dining room. Attach a note to the tablecloth with a safety pin. Identify the cloth size, number of table leaves it covers and number of matching napkins.

Or another suggestion is to take a picture of the tablecloth. On the back of the photograph, indicate the size (or how many leafs this tablecloth needs) and how many napkins. Perhaps get a double set of photographs on these. One set is attached to the tablecloth, the other set put with your recipes.

Tupperware

Tupperware or Rubbermaid products that have a top and a bottom pose a special problem because they need to be matched. At the suggestion of my husband, we have started to store the Tupperware with the bowl and the top sealed together. This takes a little more room but we have found that it works. Before storing them, make sure:

1. You have eliminated those pieces that were broken, deformed or didn't have a mate.

2. You are careful after washing the bowls to ensure that there is no moisture in the bowl when the cover is sealed.

Once a year, dump all the Tupperware on the floor with the covers. Match the covers and bowls. If there is no cover, give the bowl to charity or identify the bowl in some fashion that it was cover-less, or save if for a year, then donate to charity, or use it someplace else in the house where it doesn't need a lid.

Think about limiting the sizes of the containers. Select only three sizes: a small size, a medium size and large size. You don't need to have 32 different sizes. Nothing says it has to be a perfect fit for the contents. For replacing Tupperware, call 800-858-7221.

Chapter 2—Clutter Bug's Keys to Success

1. Put things where you use them.

2. Consider renting items of infrequent use instead of buying.

3. Match parts to pieces. Do you have everything?

4. Use pictures to identify objects.

5. If you don't know what it is, toss it.

Clutterology

GETTING RID OF CLUTTER AND GETTING ORGANIZED!

CHAPTER 3

J. Kuhl

If Tarzan Never Had A Beard—Where Did He Shave?

The bathroom, which is probably the smallest room of the house, is also the most frequently used room by a large number of people. This makes life interesting and organizationally challenging.

Cleaning Supplies

What cleaning supplies are kept in the bathroom? There are two theories on where to store cleaning supplies.

The first is to have a central location. When it is time to clean, you go and get the supplies and take them to where you are cleaning.

The other is to have the supplies where they are needed. Which means that the glass cleaner, tile cleaner, bowl cleaner, etc. would be stored in the bathroom.

What works for you? Are you a spur of the moment, clean as you go person? Buy two (or however many you need) of everything and store them in the locations where they will be used. Or would buying two of everything now mean there is twice as much that you don't use?

Eliminate—are you keeping some super fancy designer cleaners that don't work any better than the basic stuff?

Is there a way to either combine (reduce) cleaners (not pouring the ammonia into the vinegar) or instead is there an all-purpose cleaner that would work on two or more surfaces?

Counter Tops

Use containers to put similar, small items in (makeup, shoe polish, etc.). (See page 29.) Do you find yourself having to put the cover to the hair spray or shaving cream back on? Why? What's the purpose of the cap after purchasing it? What's the function? Is it still important? Toss it out! **Change your environment.**

Decorations

Get rid of anything that doesn't need to be there. Decorations on the back of the toilet look nice, but don't offer anything to the function of the room. Silk flowers, etc. need to be cleaned and take up space.

Entertainment

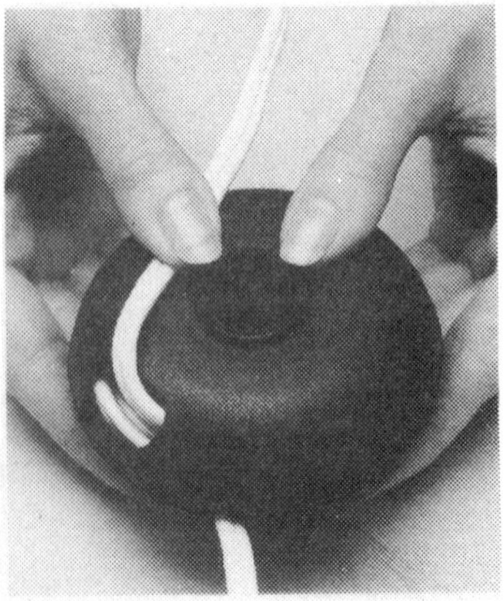

Is there some form of entertainment in your bathroom? Radio, cassette or CD? Is it sitting on the counter? Would it be possible to change the size (make it smaller)? Could a shelf be installed on the wall where the unit could sit? Have special containers been used to hold the tapes or CDs? Take a rubber band, a twist tie (from the trash liners) or even a wire wrap and neaten up the electrical cord. Lillian Vernon has this available (see page 47 for contact information).

Hamper

Does the hamper in the bathroom work for you? Do the clothes get into the hamper? If not, why not? Is the lid too difficult to get off and to put back on? Is the lid broken? Yes? Then it is time to fix it (or simplify it—take it off). Are there more clothes than hamper? Then get a larger container. (See page 104.)

Kid's Toys

Kids (and many adults) love to have their toys in the bathtub. For kids, bring toys to the bathtub is to encourage them to stay in the water longer. After awhile, it is difficult enough to get them out of the bathroom.

Look at the number and type of toys that you have provided the child in the bathroom. Is it a couple or is it an entire toy box? Is it possible to reduce the number of toys to just a couple? Or only provide a couple and rotate the toys so they seem new.

Where is the best place to store the toys? In the tub, under the sink or elsewhere. Find a place that works for you—be creative in your thinking.

Makeup

In the past couple of years, the shelf-life of cosmetics has become a factor of importance. In general, listed below are the guidelines:

Keep blush and eye shadow up to two to three years. If exposed to too much moisture (gee, the whole bathroom is filled with moisture), the product's surface may harden and the color may change.

Keep eye and lip pencils. Up to three years. If you're suspicious, sharpen the end away.

Face powder is good for up to six months. Dampness is face powder's worst enemy. When you're applying it, try sprinkling some powder onto a clean surface or a facial tissue then dipping the brush in this loose powder, instead of dipping it directly into the container.

Liquid Foundation stays blended and creamy for two years, while ingredients in long-lasting formulas tend to break down after just one year. Replace it if it is separated or has a clay-like smell. Keep it in the refrigerator to lengthen its life.

Lipsticks are good for two to three years or until it makes your lips burn or dry consistently. The first sign of spoilage could be an odor or a change in color when applied. Transfer-resistant lip color is usable only one to two years.

Keep sponges for up to one week and wash sponges daily with an antibacterial soap and let air-dry.

This is the most perishable product in your cosmetic bag. Mascara should be replaced every three to six months, or you run the risk of an eye infection. If it begins to dry up and a crust develops on the wand, toss it. Toss it sooner if it smells funny or its consistency is too thick or dry. Never share your mascara with anyone else or use saliva to thin it.

Nail polish is good for one year or until polish gets thick or separates and/or looks streaky. Store in the refrigerator.

Sunscreen is good for up to one year. If it has a funny smell, becomes runny or has been sitting in direct sunlight or a hot car, get rid of it.

Male vs. female

The battle of the sexes is very well defined in the bathroom—or is it? I was surprised to find how similar we are.

While traveling, I had forgotten my razor to shave my leg. My husband offered to loan me his. My mouth dropped open and I said, "I can't do that." Being very astute (he's been to my seminar), he asked "Why?" As I tripped over my tongue trying to remember why a female couldn't use a male's razor, I remembered the television sit coms. The man emerged from the bathroom with small pieces of toilet paper on his face which was stopping the bleeding from all the nicks his razor produced after his girlfriend used it to shave her legs.

Trusting my husband as I do, I went ahead and used his razor. Surprise! After he shaved, there was no toilet paper on his face. Another myth vanished.

Are there differences between male and female razors? Sometimes. Other times, the only difference is that one razor is black and the other razor is pink. Many times, the only difference is the price tag. Test for yourself to see what works.

Here is a suggestion that Mike came up with from his boot camp days in the Marines. In a large family (you define large), give each person a container. All of their toiletries must fit within the container and be carried back and forth from the bathroom to the bedroom. This is a good suggestion for a small bathroom (assuming that the bedroom is any bigger). This is also a nice way of setting limits. (See page 19.)

Medicine Cabinet

One of the smallest locations is the medicine cabinet and the most usual location for makeup, supplies, soaps, medicines, or toothpaste. Do you see daylight between the tallest object and the next shelf? There are now removable/redesignable units available to make space more effective. (See the catalog listed on 47.)

Check the expiration date on the medicines. Toss out medicines that are past the expiration date.

When purchasing medicine for a cold (or a specific illness), note that most medicines are effective if the whole supply is used until gone.

Mark the date that you purchased that bottle of aspirins and see how long it will take to consume. (See page 12.)

A caution about taking medicines out of the original packaging and placing it in smaller, more convenient containers. When your travel plans take you across International borders, to help clear customs with a little more ease, don't change the medicines to another container—even if the bottle is almost empty. If the inspectors can't identify the pills, they may retain you longer than you would like. Check with pharmacists to get a travel size.

If you are looking for a place to start de-cluttering your life, the medicine cabinet is a great place. It is small, has limited choices and when done, looks like you have accomplished something.

More Room In The Bathroom?

Install a shelf over the bathroom door. This is a great place for towels (assuming you can reach it easily). A word of caution, watch how much weight you place on the shelf. You don't want it to tumble down because of too much weight.

39% of us peek in our host's bathroom cabinet

from Statistics about Americans

Look under the vanity and at the space over the tank. Do you see any extra space there? Install some space saving devices.

Look at the size of your bottles, and tubes. Can you make it smaller by putting it in smaller container? Reduce the number of your inventory.

Use suction cups to place objects (perfume, decorations) on the mirror or on the tiles. There are some mighty huge suction cups at drug stores, hardware stores and even at stores like Target, K-Mart or Wal-Mart.

Here are an assortment of catalogs that have products to help you get organized.

Frontgate
9180 Le Saint Drive
Fairfield, OH 45014
800-626-6488

Get Organized!
600 Cedar Hollow Road
PO Box 1776
Paoli PA 19301-0921
800-803-9400

Good Idea! Catalog (The)
PO Box 955
Vail CO 81658-0955

Lillian Vernon Corporation
Virginia Beach, VA 23479
800-285-5555
www.lillianvernon.com

Home Silvo
3201 Tollview Drive
Rolling Meadows, IL
60008-3705

Home Trends
1450 Lyell Avenue
Rochester NY 14606-9930
716-254-6520

Solutions Inc.
PO Box 6878
Portland OR 97228
800-543-8633

Perfumes

There seems to be perfume in everything these days—makeup, soap, shampoo, toilet paper, etc. More and more people are allergic to perfumes.

One of the most common personal issues for people who are living together (at a college dorm or in an apartment complex) are complaints about the perfume other people are wearing and the smell of cooking.

When I was growing up, each Sunday we sat near a window in church because my dad's allergies were upset by the ladies' perfumes. Perfume made his life miserable.

I recently received an announcement to a conference. At the bottom of the registration form was this statement: Seminar is scent-free. Please do not wear fragrances. A sign of the future?

Perfume also has a shelf-life of about two years once it has been opened. So once you open the bottle, continue to use it. Store in a cool location.

Is it possible to reduce the number of perfumes that you use? Select one or two of your favorites. Reduce the size, buy the smallest bottle instead of the largest. Do you need or want it? Suggestion—perfume makes a great re-cycling gift idea!

Reading Material

Is the bathroom a place where reading materials collect? By placing reading material in the bathroom, are you actually encouraging people to linger in the bathroom? How big is the stack of reading material? Is it leaning over? Yes? Then reduce the number!

Talk to a local fix-it person or carpenter. I have seen some great looking built-in magazine racks that are cut between the studs of the wall. When we priced them, they were under $100. About the same price as some decorative containers!

Soap

Does the guest soap in your home gather dust more than it is used to lather guests' hands? Aren't those little bars of soap in the shapes of swans, Christmas trees, and shells cute? After sitting in a puddle of water for a while or after being used a few times, it is difficult to identify the shape of the soap.

Does the guest soap in your home add something? Yes? Great. If you didn't put out guest soap in your home, would you have fewer guests (please explain this to me—is this a good thing or a bad thing)? If you are putting out soap just for guests, start with a fresh bar, and when they leave, use it yourself.

If you are using bar soap and would like to make it last longer (while using it, unlike guest soap which gathers dust) here is a little trick. Unwrap the soap and let it *air out* before you use it.

By unwrapping the soap and letting the soap be exposed to the air, the soap doesn't melt as fast.

Use a crystal dish or candy dish as a soap dish!

Here are a few suggestions for setting limits on the soap in your home. How many bathrooms do you have? What is the average length of time that a bar of soap (or a bottle of soap) lasts for your family? How often do you go shopping?

How much money is saved between buying a case from the discount store vs. in-store prices? (Be sure to include the cost to store the case of soap, add a factor in for waste, and also add in the cost for you to dust the soap). (See page 34.)

Mike loves to collect the bars and bottles of soaps from the hotels when he is traveling. The price of a bar of soap is approximately 34¢ per ounce. However, he gets a great deal of satisfaction by bringing this stuff home. Me, I would rather not pack and carry it, so I leave it.

I have a question (which I don't have an answer for). What happens to all that soap in the hotel that is used once and then disappears when the maid service comes in?

Toothpaste

No, I am not going to debate whether the toothpaste cap should be on or off. However, does your family have several different tubes of toothpaste in use at the same time? Is it possible for everyone to share the same brand? If not, and the room in the bathroom is limited, have the individuals keep the toothpaste with their supplies.

Towels

I have always been confused by the number and description of towels—guest towel, finger towel, hand towel, and bath towel.

What are they all for? I am still asking myself what finger towels are for? Only drying a finger?

First, ask yourself (and your family) what do you use it for, why do you use it, in other words, what's important?

I found that I needed only two sizes of towels—hand towels and bath towels. My towels last for about ten years. Just recently, Mike asked for a wash cloth because *now* he needed it.

Growing up, I would get upset with the towels in the bathroom for a couple of reasons. First, they were so thin that it took a couple of towels just to get dry. Secondly, because everyone shared them after my dad would wash his hands and then wipe the dirt off on the towel, I didn't like to dry my face with that towel. It was very important to me to have my own!

If there are several members in a family, color coding the towels by individuals could be useful. (See page 104.)

Where are you keeping your extra towels—in the hall closets? What if you have just taken a shower and there is no towel in the bathroom, are you going to run out into the hall to get it? Consider storing the extra towels in the bathroom.

How big of a towel do you need? Mike and I found that for exercising we didn't need **that** big of towel. Not as large as a bath towel, but a hand towel was too small. So we took a super size bath towel (beach towel size) and had the tailor cut it into thirds. Just right! Have it monogrammed so if it is accidentally left behind, it is easy to identify.

As a small child, I loved to clean the bathroom. It was just my size, and after I was done, it looked clean. Teach your children from three years on how to pick up after themselves. Toys, after bathing, are put away once again. I like to use dishpans and kitty litter pans for containers. (See page 16.)

When the shower is used, clean off the shower doors as you are stepping out. Wash the tub as the water is draining and it is easy!

Trash Cans

Is there more trash than can? If so, super size the container. There is nothing that says we have to have a bathroom size container in the bathroom. Look for the size and shape that will fit in the space that you have, whether that is under the sink or between the bathtub and the toilet.

Use It To The End

Whether it is soap, medication, shampoo or vitamins, use the product until it is empty. I have known people to move from place to place, house to house, home to home with bottles and containers half or 3/4 empty! Or built entire additions onto the house for things half used! When my brother and I moved (we were living together for awhile while in college) he packed a huge box of empty cleaning supply containers—no, not the super good janitorial size, but the supermarket ones (that didn't work). Just one to a box!

Chapter 3—Clutter Bug's Keys to Success

1. It's easy to clean around nothing.

2. Change the size of containers to work for you (smaller or larger).

3. Decorations should have a purpose.

4. Not everything we hear on television is true.

5. Label bottles to track how long it took before it was consumed.

Clutterology

GETTING RID OF CLUTTER AND GETTING ORGANIZED!

CHAPTER 4

The Prodigal Sock

Did Sleeping Beauty Snore?

The bedroom is another room that in recent years has taken on a life of it's own. An office, a movie theater, a dressing room, a closet, a reading room and a place to sleep are just a few of it's uses.

First consideration—what is it used for? We use our bedroom for sleeping—only. We do not read in bed, eat or watch television. There are different places in the house for those activities.

As a child growing up, I had my own room that had my desk. All my homework was done at my desk. Now that we have a home office, I have no problem working in my office. I go to my desk and get down to work.

Bed Linens

January is White Sale Month. Back in the olden days, most people spent their money on Christmas gifts. The retailers, feeling the pinch of slow sales created the January White Sales to get people back to shopping.

How many sheets do you need? How often do you need to change them?

I was taught to change the sheets once a week. Coming from an agricultural environment, changing the sheets that often was necessary. Now living in the city where we take a shower once a day, do the sheets need to be changed weekly?

If you want to change the sheets, do the fitted sheet and the top sheet and the pillowcases need to be changed? Only wash that which is necessary. Sheets will last longer; you'll use less soap, water, and the washing machine will have a longer life.

Are all the beds in your home the same size? Can you make all the beds the same size? If there are different sizes, perhaps use different colors to indicate the sheet size (see page 104). How many sets of sheets do you need? Two? As one is removed from the bed, the clean sets make up the bed. In the olden days (whenever that was), the beds had to be aired out because of the materials that the mattresses were made out of (corn stalks, feathers, etc.). This is not necessarily true anymore.

How long do your sheets last? Ours have lasted ten years and counting—well, the top sheet is still good, the bottom fitted sheet was replaced. One suggestion from a seminar participant was to buy new sheets every two years to eliminate boredom.

This is a question I wish the teachers had explained to me in home economics class, how long do you keep mattress pads? How can you tell if it is *old*?

What is the purpose of a comforter in your home? Is the comforter used to add decoration when the bed is made? Is your bed made more times than it is not? Do other people see the made bed? If not, do you get a sense of satisfaction from knowing it looks good? Do you find yourself spending more time making the bed than you wish? Are you removing the comforter at night just to replace it in the morning?

Does the cute bed set have a duster? Do you like the duster? Why is it called a duster in the first place? So that dust would be stopped from finding a home under the bed. Does the duster just add more work?

For small kids (I'm not talking about age), consider using a sleeping bag or a sleeping bag style for them. Find one that is easy to wash. No need to worry about sheets (well maybe) but in the morning, just straighten out the sleeping bag and the bed is made.

My husband and I went to a comforter that had a rib on three sides so that we could make the bed easily. Just line up the rib to the edge of the bed and we know the comforter is straight.

The American Hotel and Motel Association has the Good Earth Keeping Campaign. According to the U.S. Environmental Protection Agency, only 3% of the Earth's water is fresh and hotels use 180 billion gallons of water each year (that's enough for more than 200 glasses of water for every person in the world). In an effort to conserve water and energy, and to minimize the release of detergents into the environment, hotel guests can have the bed remade, rather than having a new set of linens each day at participating hotels and motels. If you decide to re-use the towel, put it on the rack or on a hook. A towel not on the rack or hook means *please replace*. When the guest leaves, the sheets are changed and towels are freshly laundered.

How many pillows are needed on the bed? My husband and I need three pillows. Isn't it ironic that pillowcases typically come in twos—almost forcing us to use 2, 4 or 6 pillows? When Mike is not around, I can't have too many pillows. In hotels I request additional foam pillows, I like pillows.

How many decorative pillows are on the bed? You would give yourself more time if you simplified your life and just got rid of the darn things. If decorative brings pleasure, then by all means, keep the pillows.

Under-bed storage has always been a popular place to store items. Caution—sometimes under the bed becomes a big black pit that eats things. Before starting to store things under the bed, see if there is another location. If not, then limit the number of items under the bed. Out of sight, out of mind. Well, let's not lose our minds and forget it because we don't see it.

Closet

It is possible to sort your clothes into categories:

Everyday?
Semi-special?
Social?
Work?

Group your closet by type of clothes, such as all the jackets or all of the shirts together. Or group them together by color—black, blue, white, etc. Or put together complete outfits together on a single hanger.

I like to be able to look into my closet and see everything that I have to wear. I don't like looking back and forth between drawers and the closet. As a result, I hang (or put in the closet) as much of my clothing as possible (excluding shoes).

Hangers

How many hangers do you need? Enough to hang up the clothes in your closet would be a good answer.

Today, we have a wide variety of hanger styles. There are plastic, wood, metal, multiples and dry cleaner hangers. Pick a style that works!

Some of the dry cleaners now have a program where you can turn in hangers instead of tossing them. Ask the local dry cleaner. Or use the Yellow Pages and find another dry cleaner where it would be possible to drop off the hangers. Also, we talked to our dry cleaner and when we drop off the clothes we also provide a garment bag (we picked it up at a thrift shop for $1). Instead of covering the clothes with plastic that we immediately toss out, the clothes are placed in the garment bag. A great idea for anyone with small children because plastic bags are not a toy and sometimes children think they are because of all the colorful ink.

Clothes look fresher and last longer on soft satin or velvet padded contour hangers.

Clothes

If you are short on space, take a close look at seasonal clothes. Can they be removed to another location? Get a 55-gallon trash container (or smaller if needed) to put all your off-season clothes in. Store the container in the garage or wherever theirs room.

Does it fit? If not, give it away. Do you like it? If not, give it away. Does it need fixing? If so, get it fixed.

When do you get rid of clothes? When the article is past it's prime, you don't like it, won't use it, or have enough already.

Set a limit on the clothes. This is not depravation, this is extravaganza! We have the freedom to choose how many clothes we need.

How can you tell if the fabric is worn out? Has the material become shiny? Does the material wrinkle when you take a handful and squeeze it for a few seconds, and then the wrinkles don't brush out? If your husband's pant pocket shows the wallet and the wallet is not there, is it time to get rid of it? Can you see through the fabric? Has the material started to create balls? Are there stains that have become permanent?

How many clothes do you need? Growing up, I remember the children's song, "Monday is the day we wash our clothes, wash our clothes, wash our clothes ... Tuesday, iron our clothes." If we wash weekly, do we need more clothes than a week's worth?

Do you find that the tie belt of the robe keeps coming untied or the front of the robe doesn't stay closed, showing way more than you intended to show? Sew it up!

Whenever we purchase clothes, we ask the question of why do we need this? If it is for replacement, then when we get home, that *old* piece of clothing goes to Goodwill. (But ... it's still good for painting the house.) How many of those clothes are needed?

If you want the clothes, that's fine—that is a good reason. Don't pretend it is for another reason.

Nylons

Dupont developed nylon between two of their laboratories at the same time—London and New York. The product name was a combination of the two cities—NY and LONdon.

An easy way to tell if there is a run is to knot the leg with the run immediately when you take it off. Then, if you accidentally put it back into the drawer, you know immediately that it is not wearable.

There are lingerie bags available to store nylons in. If you don't want to go to the cost, zip-lock bags also work. If you find a brand, style, color, etc. of nylon that you like—cut off (or tear) the label and slip into the bag. Also, sometimes if a style doesn't work, I make a notation on the label that the color just didn't look right, they didn't last long enough, etc.

The women of the British Royal family have dressers. In addition to laying out the Royals' clothes for an engagement, the dresser is also responsible for listing what clothes (and accessories) were worn to what engagement. If you look at photographs of the royal women, it is possible to determine the engagement by the clothes and accessories.

Although Queen Elizabeth II is the richest woman in the world (estimated in the billions), she is also very frugal. She wears her dresses many times. After a dress is no longer suitable for public engagements, it is worn to dinner (when a few friends are invited over—say 30 to Balmoral Castle).

The Queen has never thrown or given away any of her clothes. In fact, all of her old clothes are stored at Buckingham Palace. Buckingham has over 300 rooms. Wouldn't it be a pity if she had to move out because she needed more closet room?

Diana would have her clothes reconstructed so that they would reflect the current style instead of buying yet another dress. She even did this on a couple of her maternity dresses.

Diana solved the old clothes problem in a couple of very modern ways. After she wore her clothes a number of times she would give them to family and friends. A unique situation for Diana was weddings. Because the bride is center stage, Diana did not want to do anything to upstage the bride, so she always wore low-key (old) clothes to weddings. However, since weddings are family events, many of her family and friends were there. Because they wanted to dress up, they wore Diana's old clothes. More than once Diana got a case of the giggles when she sat in the congregation and looked around and saw her clothes!

Diana also gave her clothes to charity. She was able to do a little more for those charities than we can with our donations, but the idea is the same.

Furniture

Installing a new closet system can sometimes even double closet space—especially in older homes and apartments where closet space is not used efficiently.

Two top franchisers of closet systems are the California Closet Co., and The Closet Factory. Both firms have systems to organize home offices, garages, basements, pantries and other areas of living space.

We put in a closet organizer which we bought at a hardware store and installed ourselves. The organizer was so practical that my husband found that he didn't need the dresser in the bedroom. We moved the dresser to the dining room. We love it there. We use the dresser as a serving buffet. The drawers are a great size for silverware and place mats. The bonus was that the furniture matched. Our taste from one room to the next is very similar.

When purchasing furniture, take a close look at how the furniture is designed. Are there a lot of nooks and crannies? The fancier the furniture, the more time and effort it will take to clean and care for it. Look for straight legs, limited amount of scrolling, etc.

How many things do you have on top of your **dresser**? Set a limit. What is the purpose of the dresser top? Is it a knickknack shelf? If so, load it up. Is it a staging area for dressing, keeping jewelry, keeping hatpins, etc? Then remove those items that don't assist that task. The walls work wonderfully for decorating and are more practical.

Is the **nightstand** a *catch all* for everything? Is it possible to simplify or reduce the items on the bed stand?

Many nightstands have a lamp. Could down lights (spots) be installed over the bed? This is a great solution assuming that the furniture in the bedroom is not moving around that often or that the lights can be changed (re-directed) after installation.

A **clock** on a nightstand is also a popular location (a necessity). Would it be possible to move the clock to the dresser? Is there room on the dresser top? What is the clock for? Telling time or is it an alarm? Can the size of the clock be reduced? Would a watch work? Is the clock also a radio? Does it work? Does it get used?

The **walls** are also considered a part of the furniture. What is on the walls? Do the decorations provide pleasure or are they functional? Would it be possible to get rid of a couple of the items? Could the size be reduced?

Jewelry

Jewelry is another item that is personal and often has sentimental value. Once a year (or so) I go through my jewelry box (which is a container) and match the back of earrings to earrings and match the pairs of earrings together.

We have a jeweler that we use regularly. They provide batteries for watches, or gold plating for a broach that is starting to show its wear. I wear gold jewelry, not silver. There were a couple of pieces of silver jewelry that I loved but wasn't wearing, I had them gold plated—now I wear them all the time. **Change your environment**.

When checking jewelry, see if it is:

- Worn out. This is more for costume jewelry. Use your judgment. I am frequently too close to the situation and have to ask Mike if he thinks that the jewelry is past its prime. Costume jewelry isn't expected to last forever.

- Broken or mismatched pieces. If possible, fix the broken pieces or it is time to get rid of them? Keep the mismatched pieces for a short period of time. If you are unable to find the missing piece in that period of time, get rid of the piece. I have a small sack (or plastic bag) where I keep my mismatched pieces. Then when I want a new piece of jewelry, I can take this sack down to the jewelry store and trade them in for another piece.

- Can you create a new use of a piece such as wearing a tuxedo jewel in lieu of a tie? Wearing an earring as a button cover or a broach?

- Keepsakes—not worn but has sentimental value. Can these be put in a different place or changed (frame them)? (See page 130.)

I use a Tupperware container to hold my jewelry. I can use the smaller containers to sort (compartmentalize) earring, necklaces, etc. The container is kept in a draw where I have easy access. When traveling, I just put a cover on a container and off we go.

When you pass by a jewelry store, have the jeweler steam clean the jewelry that you are wearing.

The Royals are also notorious for multipurpose use of jewelry. Many of the broaches are also a part of a necklace. The tiara can have the diamonds taken out and the emeralds put it. Diana once used a choker as a headband.

Purses and Briefcase

When you leave the house in the morning or go to the grocery store, are you carrying your whole life with you? Do you need to?

Take everything out of your purse, pockets and briefcase. Do the *I Might Need It Someday Exercise* (see page 19). Especially if you find yourself saying, "I carry it because my husband, my wife, my children, my co-workers might need it." Of course they don't need it! If they really, really did, they would be carrying it themselves instead of depending on you! What's the worst thing that could happen if you didn't bring it?

What do you use? What do you need? Can it be smaller? What could be stored in another location? Like the ashtray of your car? What don't you need? More and more credit cards are going to a single credit/debit card and major department stores only need your driver's license and their computer for identification.

Reading Materials

Do you use your bedroom for reading? Is there equipment to store your reading material (baskets, bookcase, boxes, or a trash can)? If magazine reading is a part of this pile, locate a trash can next to your bed so that you can toss the finished materials into the container.

Shoes

How many pairs of shoes does a person need? In my case, none (I don't wear pairs!!) Many times, Madison Avenue and the temptation of the department stores have lured us into buying more than we need. Take a look at the clothes in the closet. Now match clothes to shoes. How many pairs are required? Start with the basics, how many black pairs of flat shoes are needed? Probably only one or two.

The average American woman owns at least 30 pairs of shoes; the passionate collector owns in the hundreds.

One of the early lessons I learned about crutches is that if I wanted to change heel height, I had to change the height of the crutches (wood crutches are not adjustable). No longer could I just kick off my 3" heel at the front door or the crutches would come up to my lower lip.

I had to devise a system so that at approximately the same time as I put on my shoe, I would have access to my crutches. So, I store my shoes under my bed (with a roll out container) and the crutches are just a hop away!

For longer use, letting the shoes air over night or wear them every other day gives the shoes a chance to breathe. Is there one color in your wardrobe that you have more of than another?

Do you have a pair of shoes that you don't wear because they are the wrong color or you don't have any clothes that they go with? Dye the shoes black.

Above and beyond the basics—how many pairs of shoes do you want? One or two pairs, but how many more than that? What's the worst thing that could happen if you only have six pairs of shoes? It makes deciding a lot easier and a lot faster.

Some people love shoes. That's OK if it is their only obsession. But if everything is an obsession, take a closer look at the root of this need to keep everything.

When sorting through the shoes, look at the condition of the shoes. Are they worn out? Look at the heel, is the heel over-run or worn-out? Is there a gouge in the shoe that can't be fixed? Do the shoes hurt? Get them out of the closet.

Once I bought a custom made shoe from the Queen's shoemaker—Lobbs (this was one time I was very happy for only one foot—at those prices, I couldn't afford two). We created a shoe that worked for me—a wide heel (which creates more stability than a thin heel) of medium height, the heel was centered on the shoe creating even more stability and there was a *sand paper* bottom so that on wet tile or on snow, I wouldn't fall as easily.

The Royals know how important shoes are, especially for as long as they have to stand. If you were to look at a picture of Queen Elizabeth and her sister Princess Margaret, one way to tell the two apart is that Princess Margaret wears open toed shoes while the Queen wears closed toe shoes.

Shoes: A Celebration of Pumps, Sandals, Slippers & More
by Linda O'Keeffe
Price: $11.95 Paperback 512 pages
ISBN: 0761101144

88 percent of all women buy shoes that are one size too small for them.

Ties

Although men don't have the range of clothing styles that women have to contend with, they do have something that women don't have to deal with—ties.

Pull all the ties out of the closet (or wherever their home is). Are there any ties that are out of style? Give them to charity. Are there ties that don't work—too short, too long, the wrong color? Give to charity. Are there ties that just aren't worn? Give to charity.

After the tie comes back from the dry cleaners, examine it for stains, frays, fuzz balls, or fading. If present, this is a good indication that the life of that tie has passed.

How many ties are enough? 12 ties if you're average. That gives a little over two weeks of workdays with a different tie. Some industries (legal) have very expressive ties. Some industries don't use ties that often (technology).

The Book of Ties
by Francois Chaille and Jean-Claude Colban
Price: $45 Hardcover 180 pages
ISBN: 2080135686
Full history, fabrics, and maintaining a tie collection.

Chic Simple: Shirt and Tie
by Kim Johnson Gross, Jeff Stone and Michael R. Solomon
Price: $13.95 Hardcover 95 pages
ISBN: 067942766X
This book is about paring down to the essentials, owning less, spending less, and looking better.

Under Garments

Setting Limits. How much you need could be based on how often we do laundry. What if we have more than we need? Lay out all your garments so that it is easy to compare. Do any under garments have elastic that no longer does it's job or only does a feeble job? Fire it. Eliminate the two worst of the group. If your mother were to wash your clothes, would any piece cause you embarrassment? Is it discolored, yellowed or stretched out? If so, get rid of it.

In our home, socks aren't that big a deal. My husband had a wonderful suggestion (men can do this a little easier than women). He found a pair of socks that he likes and bought two dozen pairs. He never has more than one missing sock, or and then it usually shows up, or sometimes, I inherit it!

My brother always wore work boots or cowboy boots. He never had a matched set of socks in his bachelor life. No need! He wore mismatched socks and the boots covered them up.

Sort through the socks. Are there socks that are worn out, threadbare or mismatched? Do your socks tend to slip down? Get rid of them!

Neatnix Organizers
3979 Lockridge St
San Diego CA 92102
619-266-2662 or 800-683-6328 or 619-266-1334 fax
Neatnix has a variety of practical, useable organizing products. There most popular are: wire basket or drawer organizers (no tools needed and fits **all** sizes), jewelry stax™, and sox box.

Shoe Repair Shop

One of the best sources to locate in your community is a good shoe repair shop. Now, it is not necessarily for fixing shoes (although that is a good idea), but they do a whole lot more like: fixing and repairing luggage, belts, purses, shoes, briefcases, and leather coats.

Ask yourself this: Is the bedroom the best place to store your clothes? Where do you like to dress and undress? Is it a bathroom? Is there another room available for a dressing room? Be creative in your thinking.

Tailor

One of the first things that I do with new clothes is to go to the tailor. I have pockets put into all my clothes. Frequently, I don't carry a purse but I need a place to carry my keys. Or I need the hem shortened or lengthened.

Hats

Cowboy or felt hats can be cleaned at the dry cleaners. Talk to the cleaners to see if they can block the hat. Or check the Yellow Pages for stores that sell Western wear or a tack store (tack is horse equipment but many times these stores sell people equipment also). They may clean or service the hats, or know who does.

The Cowboy Hat Book
by William Reynolds and Ritch Rand
Price: $19.95 Paperback 95 pages
ISBN: 0879056592
How to choose a hat, measure properly for fitting, clean it, store it, travel with it, discussion of *hat hair* and more.

Chapter 4—Clutter Bug's Keys to Success

1. Know your habits and match supplies to it (wash weekly—clothes for a week).

2. Simply whenever possible.

3. Redesign to fit your needs.

4. Spend an hour cleaning, sorting, etc but save the last five minutes to clean and pick up.

Clutterology

GETTING RID OF CLUTTER AND GETTING ORGANIZED!

CHAPTER 5

Don't pass this deal up!
You need a new credit card!
Actually, 3 more cards!
Subscribe to us!
Our cause needs you and your money!
Everything marked down 50-75%!
HEY, You!

The Postman Always Rings Twice and Carries a Big Bag!

For years now, experts have been saying that technology will eventually create *paperless offices*. Well, statistics show that this isn't happening anytime soon.

Junk Mail

Junk mail (unwanted solicitations) can be slowed down—dramatically!

1. Go down to the Post Office (or use stamps by mail) and get 15 postcards.

2. On the back of the postcards write:

> Please remove my name from mailing lists databases.
>
> ______________________________
> *(Signature Required)*
>
> ______________________________
> First Name   Last Name
>
> ______________________________
> Street Address
>
> ______________________________
> Suite/Apartment No.
>
> ______________________________
> City   State   Zip+4
>
> Thank you for your assistance and cooperation in this matter.

3. Send a postcard to each of the addresses below. These companies or associations maintain databases (lists) which rent your name, address and telephone number.

The trick here is that you must include each name variation to your address (including misspellings). They maintain your name on their **delete list** between two and five years. You'll see results in about three months.

ADVO-Systems, Inc.
List Service Supervisor
239 West Service Road
Hartford, CT 06120-1280

American Express
Customer Service
200 Vesey Street - Tower C
New York NY 10285

Carol Wright Gifts
340 Applecreek Road
Lincoln NE 68528-1501
402-474-2018

Cox Direct Operations Dept
6030 North US 301
Elm City NC 27822
919-236-4301 press 6131

Database America
Consumer Compilation Dept
100 Paragon Drive
Montvale NJ 07645-0419
800-223-7777

Donnelley Marketing, Inc.
Data Base Operations
1235 N Avenue
Nevada IA 50201-1419
515-382-5441

Dun & Bradstreet
Customer Service
899 Easton Avenue
Bethlehem PA 18025
800-333-0505

Harte Hanks Direct Marketing
List Maintenance
10 Alco Place
Baltimore, MD 21227-2090
410-247-0666

Mail Preference Service
Direct Mail Association
PO Box 9008
Farmingdale NY 11735-9008
212-768-7277 or
202-955-5030 ext 1888

Metromail Corporation
Consumer Services
901 West Bond
Lincoln, NE 68521
800-228-4571

Money Mailer
14271 Corporate Drive
Garden Grove, CA 92843
714-265-4100

R. L. Polk & Company
Name Deletion File
List Compilation and Development
26955 Northwestern Hwy
Southfield, MI 58034
800-873-7655

Val-Pak Coupons
Address Information Dept
8575 Largo Lakes Drive
Largo FL 33773
800-237-2871
(have the envelope when calling)

Telemarketers

Get on the **do not call list**. Every telemarketer must maintain a do not call list according to FTC law (excluding charity/non profit). If they violate this within 12 months, a lawsuit can be filed for $500 per violation. Tell the telemarketer:

1. Add your name to their Do Not Call List.
2. Send you a copy of their Do Not Call Policy.

To reduce the amount of national advertising calls you receive at home contact the following companies. After a few months, the amount of advertising calls you receive from national marketers such as credit card and magazine subscription companies will be reduced. Some local organizations and charities may not participate.

American Telephone Fundraisers
USPS Kilbuck Branch
1001 California Ave
PO Box 99311
Pittsburgh, PA 15233-9998

Private Citizen
PO Box 233
Naperville IL 60566
800-288-5865
Remove you +1500 mail and phone lists for a charge

MCI Consumer Affairs
800-289-6722
Request a copy of their Do Not Call policy.

Telephone Preference Services
Direct Marketing Association
PO Box 9014
Farmingdale, NY 11735-9014
212-768-7277

California Public Utilities Commission
Consumer Affairs Branch
505 Van Ness Avenue
San Francisco CA 94102
800-555-7809
To have California's power industry, electric service providers (ESPs) add your name or business to the ***Do Not Call Me*** lists, send your request in writing to the above address. Any ESP, which solicits a customer on the list more than once, must pay $25 to the customer for each contact.

Pre-Approved Credit Card Applications

Ever wondered why you get pre-approved credit applications? Because, your credit bureau sells your name and address. Writing to the following companies will help to reduce this paper flow.

Equifax Options Opt-Out
PO Box 740123
Atlanta GA 30374-0123
888-567-8688

Experion Opt-Out (was TRW)
Target Marketing Services
701 TRW Parkway
PO Box 919
Allen, TX 75013
888-567-8688

Trans Union Opt-Out
TransMark, Inc.
555 West Adams Street
Chicago IL 60661
800-680-7293

Tips and Tricks

- Catalog companies will take as long as 6-9 months before your name is removed from their mailings. They print the mailing labels and/or catalogs in mass quantities.

- Contact all the organizations whose mailings you receive and would rather not receive.

- When placing catalog orders, check the box (or make special notation on the order form) that this is for *in-house use only.*

- If you have any concerns about not getting a catalog you want, keep a copy of the phone number. Then, if you want to be placed back on the list, call them.

> ***The average total number of mail pieces sent or received per household increased to 25 pieces per week in 1995.***
>
> ***United States Postal Service***

- Don't fill out warranties, registration forms or participate in surveys. Your name will then be circulated among the telemarketing companies.

- Don't buy anything through telemarketing.

- Don't donate to charity using telemarketing. Contact the charity directly. Check if the charity is in fact associated with the telemarketer. Many telemarketing companies have scams with sound-alike company names of charities.

- If asked by a charity for a donation, check it out further. We have received e-mails and chain letters from *Make A Wish Foundation.* When I called the 800 operator, I had trouble finding the phone number, but she gave me the number of a similar name. After talking to the administrator, what I thought we would be supporting (a boy's dying wish to be in the Guinness World Book of Records for collecting the most business cards) turned out to be false. I found out that there was no such company and that this chain had started some three or four years previously and the child that it referred to had died.

- Buy hardware for screening purposes. Use your answering machine that informs telemarketers they're not welcome. Phone Butler is such a devise. The moment you identify an unwanted call, press the star key on any touchtone or cordless phone and hang up. The Phone Butler (with a British accent) politely tells the unwanted caller:

"Pardon me, this is the Phone Butler, and I have been directed to inform you that this household must respectfully decline your inquiry. Kindly place this number on your do-not call list. Good Day."

Hello, you are talking to a machine. I am capable of receiving messages. My owners do not need siding, windows, or a hot tub, and their carpets are clean. They give to charity through their office and do not need their picture taken. If you're still with me, leave your name and number and they will get back to you.

Incoming Correspondence

Pre-sort the mail for the designated person. For family members, create a location to pick up their mail (such as their place at the table). In the office, either create a location on your desk where mail awaits pick up, or create a location on their desk for incoming mail.

Sort your mail into piles: toss, read, file and to do.

Many organizers suggest that the mail be sorted over the trash can. There will always be some unavoidable junk mail. So, yes, sort over the trash can if it is not possible to get off the mailing list.

Handle the mail when **you** have time. Don't let the mail dictate to you that everything must stop. Complete the activity that you are working on. When there comes a natural break, at that point, handle the mail.

Double-Check the Addressee

Any mail that comes to your address, but is not yours, write on the envelope: **Not At This Address, Return to Sender**

Put the envelope back in the mailbox. Be sure to cover up the bar code (on the front of the envelope or the back of the envelope).

Handling the Read and File Piles

When going through a letter, read it with a highlighter in hand. Highlight the name/word/subject that this piece of paper will eventually be filed under.

Make notes on the pages as you read so you don't have to re-read the document. Sometimes the first impression may have some wording, suggestions or ideas that you might not remember or think of in the second reading.

Establish a location on the document where the *history* of this document will be located. The upper right-hand corners or upper left-hand corners are good locations.

First notation: when was this document received. This would be the date stamp if date stamping were appropriate.

Second notation: where to file the document. If in the future the document is misfiled, it can easily be re-filed. Or if the file name changes, the logical progression of the document is there.

Third notation: if certain individuals need to read the document before the document is filed, it is easy for the file clerk to see if everyone has read it before filing it.

Fourth notation: active date. How long does this document remain in the active file? Some papers don't need to be kept after a year. (See page 98 for more information.)

Fifth notation: destroy date. How long does this need to be archived?

When it comes time to clean out the files, it will be easy because all you need to do is look for documents that have only the date it was put into the file.

Skylar Smith
123 Any Place Street
Any Where, US 98765-4321
[999] 555-1212

10/01/99
Smith, Skylar
nkm
mfr
10/01/00

September 17, 1999

Your Name Goes Here
The Name of the Company You Work For
Their Street Address
City State and Always Remember the ZIP+4

Dear You:

Thank you for taking the time out of your hectic day to spend three hours on the telephone with me today. This note is just to let you know how much I really, really, really appreciated it and that I am looking forward to wasting more of your time, energy and money in the future.

Sincerely,

Skylar Smith

Enclosure: A picture of myself

Time Management Tip: When possible, consider answering routine letters on the original documents, photocopy the document for your records and send it off. They will be impressed with your quick response.

In an office environment, many times, when the mail is opened, the documentation is date stamped. Why? What is the purpose for the date stamping? Sometimes, it is simply a CYA (cover your assets). If there is no reason, don't do it.

Bills

> ***In 1993, Congress received more than 300,000,000 pieces of mail; that figure was up from 15,000,000 in 1970.***
>
> ***Adapted from Association Management***

Do you put a return address on your bills? Why? Do you think the company printed the wrong address on their envelopes—nope? That you might forget to put postage on the envelope? There are two options—either the Post Office will open the envelope and send it back to you so you can put postage on the envelope. (Is a late payment of a couple of days worth the extra effort to put the return address on all bills?) Or the Post Office will mail the letter with postage due.

Reduce the number of bills (consolidate the bills, pay off as many bills as possible or don't open any new accounts).

Cancel any credit cards that are not used on a regular basis.

Change the billing cycle. Let's say that you get paid twice a month—the 1st and the 15th. If the mortgage is due on the 1st, request that the billing date for the credit cards be the 15th. Some credit card companies will not be able to accommodate this request. Some credit card companies will have to reissue the credit card because the billing date is tied to the numbers on the credit card.

Ask that the company not include the *stuffers*—those papers that fall out when the envelope is opened. Again, some companies will be able to accommodate this request; some might not be able to.

Chapter 5—Clutter Bug's Keys to Success

1. Get removed from as many databases as possible for junk mail, telemarketers, and pre-approved credit card applications.

2. Order floresent stickers from Rounds, Miller and Association *Attention: List Manager. Please remove from your database. Thank you* which can be placed on junk mail envelopes.

3. If a telemaketer calls you, asked to be put on their do not call list and ask for a copy of their policy.

4. Check out charities before contributing.

5. Create a history corner on documentation.

Clutterology

GETTING RID OF CLUTTER AND GETTING ORGANIZED!

CHAPTER 6

The adage that says "When you die, your 'In' basket won't be empty" was certainly true for Ed.

I Know The Buck Stops Here But Why The Paperwork?

Do you spend more and more time rooting through piles muttering to yourself, "I know it's here somewhere?" Have any of your colleagues joked that your desk should be declared a disaster area?

The paper invasion overwhelms many offices. Piles of paper spread until they cover every flat surface. Soon, if steps are not taken, you will see reminders everywhere of incomplete projects, unwritten memos, and unread journals.

In an office environment, it is important to standardize. There isn't enough time to ask questions during the busy day. KISS it (**k**eep **i**t **s**hort and **s**imple).

> ***Faxes put out 30 billion pieces of paper a year.***
> ***Copiers duplicate 60 million copies an hour.***
> ***Computer printers print 2.5 million documents a second.***
>
> ***Avery Dennison***

There are four stages for filing:

1. The primary space (the area you can touch when reaching out your arms) is used for items that are used every day (stapler, telephone, pen, keyboard, and working files). Immediate use.

2. Daily (desk drawer)—secondary space (that which requires bending and stretching) are items that you need today and are used frequently.

3. Active (filing room) that area where we have to get up and go to. Items that are not used on a daily basis.

4. Inactive (storage) are those that you need to keep for a period of time.

Primary Space—Desktop

There was one boss that I heard about who insisted that all the desks in his department have a clean desktop. He wasn't talking about having the piles stacked neatly and the pencils in the pencil holder straight. He meant nothing on top of the desk. Each Friday, he would hold an inspection to see that all the desktops were clean. Typically what people did was to stuff the papers in the desk drawer just before he came around. In fact, before he transferred, maintenance was required to drill holes in his desk drawer so that the telephone could be placed in the drawer!

Take a look at the top of the desk. The objects on top are those things that are used on a **daily** basis. Look at each and every one of them and decide if they are needed. Is there an empty container (business card holder, tape dispenser, stapler, or penholder) on the desk? Reality check!! If it is empty, you don't need it on your desktop! **Change your environment**.

How often is the tape dispenser used? Daily, weekly or perhaps monthly. If it is not daily, then find another home for the tape dispenser. Reduce and simplify. I put mine in the drawer and on a small dispenser because I rarely use it.

Look at the number of cords that are around the desk. Is it possible to reduce the number of cords? See if it is possible to convert to a battery-operated unit. Test how long the battery will last. We have a battery-operated stapler that lasts over a year with daily use.

Pictures of friends and family (all 3,432) and other decorations. The purpose of the desktop is for working. A picture or two is appropriate. Can another location be found for the pictures? If there is a computer on the desk, scan the pictures and create a screen saver.

How many pens do you have on top of your desk, in your drawers and in general, around you? Do you need that many? The pens will eventually dry up, so all the savings are for naught.

Most pens are made of plastic today, so don't light the tip with a match. Pens do have a shelf-life; disposables last about two to three years, depending on the brand. Store pens horizontally at room temperature (65° to 75°F). Heat and humidity can cause leaking, and cold air may make a pen stop writing temporarily. Label and date the box. (See page 12.)

Do people keep walking off with your pens? You can train co-workers not to walk off with your stuff. Start by using a unique pen or pencil that is not supplied by the business. A hotel pen or a give away pen is good. Also, choose an ink color that is not black or blue (the more sickening the color the better). Only have the one pen out and use it. When someone comes up and asks, "Can I use your pen?" gladly offer your pen, letting them know that it's your only pen. Most of the time they will give the pen back or they will go to someone else's desk to borrow a pen. I have had people walk half way down the hall or even in the next building and then walk back with **my** pen!

Keep a second pen in the desk drawer. Often times, pens and pencils can get buried under paperwork and they become hard to find. I always choose a favorite as my primary pen. When that pen runs out of ink, then I choose a new favorite (usually the one in the drawer). Now you understand why the more unique the pen is, the easier it is to keep track of.

Order a pen holder from Rounds, Miller and Associates. Soft plastic sleeve-on-a-rope holds **any** pen or pencil. Great for those *pocketless* days or when frequently on the move. They are $4.00 each and make a great gift for you, your family or the office.

Sometimes having too many options can be confusing and a big waste of time. Instead of a couple dozen different sizes of note pads or Post-It® Notes, select only two sizes, and make those work.

Paper clips vs. Staples. There is a debate about which is better. Paper clips are good if materials are being added to or deleted from the stack.

If the paper clip comes off, we know that we are looking for more than one piece of paper. However, sometimes papers are accidentally attached to the back of the stack. We may never suspect the additional page.

Staples are good when used in the permanent file and will actually reduce the space. Paper clips are fatter than a staple. Some businesses are now using staples to establish original vs. photocopied. The original will have the staple holes in the papers.

Norwegian John Yaaler invented the first paper clip in 1899.

There are over 48 varieties of clips made in either steel or plastic.

The United States alone uses 20,000 tons of steel wire annually to manufacture paper clips.

Secondary Space—Desk Drawers

Do you have materials in your files dating back to the Nixon administration? Ask yourself these questions when reviewing documents:

- Is the information current? Old or outdated materials can take up space better used for up-to-date facts and figures.

- When will you use the materials? If you don't know now, you probably never will.

- Is the information available elsewhere? If it's on a computer disk or somewhere else where you can find it easily when you want it, then you don't need it in your files.

- What would happen if you did lose it? If nobody would care, get rid of it!

- Is the information strictly FYI? Once you've read it, you can probably toss it without danger.

- Does this paper relate to a completed or abandoned project?

- Is this an old version of the material?

An usual item that I have in my desk drawer is a kitchen towel. I keep it handy for spilled drinks, laser cartridge toner on my hands or just too much hand lotion. In other words, although it is not logical, it is sensible to have a towel in my desk drawer.

Quick Tips for Getting Started

> ***A clean desk is a sign of a cluttered desk drawer.***
>
> ***Jest for You***

1. Clear off your work surface and get ready to re-organize. Take every piece of paper off your desk. Put it all in a storage box. (Don't worry, it won't stay there for long.) Assemble the supplies you need to get organized: file folders, markers, labels, a note pad, binders, a hole punch and a stapler. Place your trash can and re-cycling container next to your pile of paper.

2. Start at the top of the pile and ruthlessly go through it piece by piece. Pick up each piece of paper, and don't put it down until you have made a decision about it. Sort all paper into project files, making up new files as necessary. Clip correspondence to be answered to the outside front of the appropriate project file, but don't stop to compose letters or memos. Your goal is to find a logical place for every piece of paper so you will know where everything is.

3. File every folder that you are not currently working on. If you have some files that require action but not urgent action, create a master *to do* list on which you write

everything that needs to be done. Then put those files away for now. Don't leave them out as reminders. They just take up space on your desk unnecessarily; makes you look disorganized, and can distract you from the task at hand.

4. Arrange the remaining files in order of priority. You may sort by deadline or by some other criteria, but keep the most important files at your fingertips. Purchase (or locate) an upright file holder to place on your desk which will keep your priority folders within arm's reach. You will be able to slip those files in and out of their appointed slots easily. Piling files in an in-basket or on the corner of your desk usually results in those files being buried by other paper that is added to the top of the pile.

5. Clip invitations and meeting announcements to your calendar or jot details on the calendar and file the papers in the follow-up tickler file. After the events have passed, throw away invitations and meeting announcements.

> ***Despite technology's early promise of more leisure time, American workers are putting in as many hours on the job as ever—and feeling rushed most of the time.***
>
> ***1998 Day-Timer® Survey***

Look closely at how you like to do things. When buying files, make sure that they are big enough for you. Some of the more inexpensive files at the department stores only open a foot or two, making filing very difficult, and tip easily.

I am finding that by having my file trays opening on the long side, I can get the paper in and out faster.

Checking Out Files

Have you ever tried to use those checkout folders when a folder is pulled out of the file? Usually what is required is that you write you name on the check our folder and date it. I don't know about you, but in my experience, when I need a folder, it is usually when the customer is on the phone, and I don't have time to write that stuff. I need it now!

An easy way to accomplish the same result is to assign a color to each person. As they walk into the file room, they grab the color card stock and slip it in as the folder is being pulled out. I went one step further. I printed on the colored card stock "This folder was checked out by Daniel Miller" in 125 point.

Another simple step to help speed up filing is to pre-sort the materials. Instead of just one in-box, create two in-boxes. A-M and O-Z. That way, there is a little step taken to break things down. Then two people can work on the filing. Don't over complicate this system.

Then each time that you (or someone else) uses that document, date it again.

Active to Inactive

A system needs to be in place for proactively moving (cleaning) the files from daily to active to inactive to disposing.

We moved on December 31. I take all of my tax records (accounts payable, accounts receivable, etc.) and move them from the active file drawer to banker/storage boxes (inactive).

Each anniversary, we spend the evening in and clean the closets. Now, this sounds crazy, but first of all, we don't like to be out on New Year's Eve when so much drinking occurs. Second, we don't worry about the project for 11½ months. Our personal and business year-end is also December 31st.

We spent three days before our move cleaning and organizing the place we were moving out of and one-day packing. It was much easier to do it that way. We were highly motivated (due to the pending deadline) and the idea of packing, lifting, carrying, unpacking and finding a new home for stuff just didn't seem like fun to us. Try it sometime!

After that year, the files go down to storage (under step storage). The under stair storage is cleaned out after we move the Christmas decorations out. Those file boxes have minimal review. We keep the important tax records and after seven years, the other papers get tossed (like credit cards statements, general correspondence, etc.).

If your office does not have the space for all the records and documentation in the filing room, then some of the records have to be stored elsewhere.

Usually this is in boxed cartons. The rules for boxing—label the box, list the contents, whose records, which department, how long must the records be kept, when were they put into storage and how soon they can be destroyed?

What date or time of the year would be best for your business? Is it the end of the year (December 31st)? Or are there a large number of individuals that take vacation the week between Christmas and New Years? Does the business have a fiscal year end? That is a good time to move the files (giving it a month or two for all the paperwork to filter down to the files). Is there a natural slow period of the business? Just after the tax season or during the summer when student help or interns can be used.

Executives spend six weeks yearly looking for files, phone numbers, and other lost or mislabeled items.

Filing Systems

Eighty percent of what most people file is never used again, according to Rachel Weiss Claret, owner of The Organizer Inc., a Colorado based business. There is only one reason to file papers—to retrieve them.

Here are some questions for every document—before it is filed:

1. Why do I want/need it?
2. Why is it significant?
3. Is it information that I already have in another file?
4. Is it timely/current?
5. Is it accurate and reliable?
6. Can I obtain it elsewhere?
7. How long do I need it?
8. What would happen if it were lost?

What would you have filed it under? If it is possible, use a computer to index this material, cross-references titles, subjects, etc.

File Folder Name	Contents	Location
Distance Learning	Letter to Brian Tracy	File room
Evening with Mike		NKM office
Hearing Impaired		MFR office
Internet Tape Project		Bookshelf
Master's Track	Database of attendees	File room
Media Kit	One-sheet	File room
NSA Correspondence	Headquarters, Stacy Kech	File room

Create a file when there are three pieces of paper for that file. Use misc. files at a minimum—people are never quite sure what could be in a misc. file and it seems that there are too many pieces of paper in misc.

Create a file (just for you or a few people—this is not for the general filing room) that has meaning to you where temporary files or papers can be placed. In the advertising industry, they create **swipe** files. Whenever they see an ad in a magazine or a direct mail piece that they like, they tear it out and file in the swipe file. This file is just for creating new ideas—not to swipe the copyrighted material. I have an **idea** file. Then after a while, I toss the papers out, but it is a place to hold the papers.

Sample Typical Categories

Action Items	Banking	Bills to Pay
Charges	Charitable Donations	Credit
Family	Health Care	Housing
Income	Insurance	Investments
Loans	Mortgage	Utilities
Tax Information or Income Taxes		

Alphabetical Filing

Alphabetical is the easiest for people to work with. The white pages of a telephone book are in alphabetical order.

However, the rules of filing under an alphabetical system become tricky. Take this test. How would you file the following?

Paper for Filing		File Paper is to be Filed
1.	Lorna M. Mitchell	
2.	Linda Frazeur-Gaugert	
3.	The Printing Press	
4.	IBM	
5.	Animal Kingdom	
6.	Gordon L. Miller, DDS	
7.	EDD	

Basic Rules for Alphabetic Filing

- A person's last name first.
- Nothing comes before something (royal_ before royals or Miller before Miller, Nancy).

- Spell business names exactly as the business itself spells it own name.
- Ignore "The" at the beginning of a name.
- Ignore the hyphen in hyphenated words.
- Follow the conventions in your office, even if they are wrong (unless you can re-train everyone else).

Numeric Filing

Numeric system works best if what you are filing already has a number assigned to it or if for any reason the files need to remain confidential. Looking at 1000 file folders and trying to find specific information just by the file folder number is impossible. Don't just develop the system because the computer likes numbers.

Numeric Filing—A Guideline
Price: $29.00 Soft cover 14 pages
ARMA (Association of Record Managers and Administrators)
ISBN: 0-933887-32-9 (Catalog No. A4531)
This guide to selection and design of numeric filing systems discusses advantages and disadvantages.

ARMA International
4200 Somerset, Suite 215
Prairie Village, KS 66208-5287
913-341-3808 or 800-422-2726 http://www.arma.org/hq

Barbara Hemphill author of *Taming the Paper Tiger* has developed a modified numeric system in conjunction with the computer. The file folder labels are already produced, so the only thing you have to do is to assign the document a number (if starting a new file) and enter the information into the computer. When filing, refer to the computer to find the corresponding numeric number.

Subject files are filed by subject. These files can get a little tricky. Does it go under National Speakers Association or Speaking? Subject files are good if the subjects are already well defined and common to the people using the system. Subject files are also good if the subjects are broader rather than narrow.

Subject Filing—A Guideline
ARMA (Association of Record Managers and Administrators)
Price: $36.00 Soft cover 47 pages
ISBN: 0-933887-29-9 (Catalog No. A4546)
Included are sections on dictionary and encyclopedic filing system arrangements, coding systems, and cross-referencing procedures.

Priority files are files that for whatever reasons are priorities to you and/or your boss. There may be no rhyme or reason but they are a priority. Sometimes certain clients or deadline dates create priority files.

Chronological files are filed by date. Often times this type of file is used in addition to or in conjunction with another filing system. Everything is filed by date. Invoices and purchase orders are typical of this type of filing system.

Geographical files are by territory, state, region or some geographical boundaries. This style is typical in sales offices.

Filing Cabinets

When will you retrieve it (daily, weekly, monthly, or yearly)? Those materials that are retrieved daily, should be placed near to where you use them. Is this beginning to sound familiar?

One area that is often over looked, but is very important, is the equipment and location used for filing cabinets. Many times, it is the left over locations that are used.

Get the best equipment you can afford. There are some very good used equipment stores. Check the equipment carefully. If a drawer sticks in the store, it will stick back at the office.

When setting up filing rooms take into consider physical reality. Filing is hard work on the body.

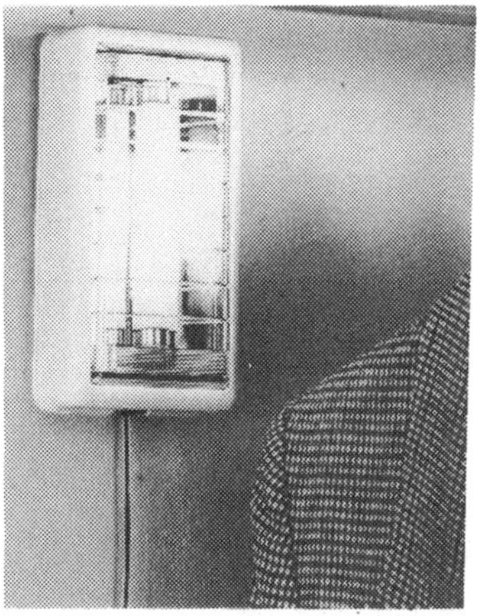

Is there a light so that the papers can be seen? If not, there are battery-operated fluorescent lights that can be purchased at hardware stores, office supply stores, or catalogs. Lillian Vernon has this product available.

Is there any air circulation or is it unbearably hot? Get a little fan to make it bearable to work.

Is there a work area for the papers? How about a table to work on? Not enough room? Folding tables work nicely.

How easy it to get to the lower or upper drawers? Provide a step stool or a chair that makes it easier to continue with the filing. Folding units are great for small spaces.

Is filing easy? How long does it take? Can you find it? Does the office have back ups? Are the files systematized?

The court system in many states will now accept 8½x11 paper. There will be fewer and fewer documents will be legal size. Don't buy any more legal filing cabinets. Try to convert the files that you do have to letter size.

E.L.F. = Eliminate Legal-size Files
ARMA (Association of Record Managers and Administrators)
Price: $8.00 Soft cover 8 pages
ISBN: 0-933887-38-8 (Catalog No. A4547)

Notebooks

Create a guide for your position and list what papers you typically handle and how/where they are filed. Ask yourself these questions: What are they? Where are they? When do I get rid of them? How do I get rid of them? How often? Legality? Worst case? Technology?

For example: Board of Director Minutes are filed in the 3-ring notebook on the bookshelf. They are kept for one year and then can be tossed into the trash. I update the book every month (one set of minutes in, one set of minutes out). I keep the original minutes because I am the office of the Corporate Secretary.

Record Retention

How long is long enough? Check with a supervisor, department head, personnel, human resources, a CPA or legal counsel to determine the correct answer for your specific business and industry.

Here's a list of generally accepted, reasonable time periods recommended for retaining your business records:

Accident reports and claims (settled cases)—7 years

Account payable and receivable ledgers and schedules—7 years

Audit reports of accountants—Indefinitely

Bank reconciliations—1 year

Bank statements—7 years

Cash books—indefinitely

Charts of accounts—indefinitely

Checks (cancelled, see exceptions below)—7 years

Checks (canceled for important payments, i.e., taxes, purchases of property, special contracts, etc.)—Indefinitely

Construction documents—indefinitely

Contracts and leases (expired)—7 years

Contracts and leases still in effect—expiration plus 7 years

Correspondence (general)—3 years

Correspondence (important)—indefinitely

Deeds, mortgages, bills of sale, titles—indefinitely

Depreciation schedules—indefinitely

Duplicate deposit slips—1 year

Electronic fund transfer documents—7 years

Employee personnel records (after termination)—7 years

Employment applications—3 years

Expense analyses and expenses distribution schedules—7 years

Financial statements (end-of-year, other months optional)—indefinitely

General and private ledgers (and end-of-year trial balance)—indefinitely

I-9s (after termination)—1 year

Insurance policies (expired)—3 years

Inventories of products, materials, supplies—7 years

Invoices to customers and from vendors—7 years

Journals—indefinitely

Licenses—indefinitely

Loan documents, notes—indefinitely

Minute books of directors and stockholders meetings, including by-laws and charter—indefinitely

Notes receivable ledgers and schedules—7 years

OSHA logs—5 years

Payroll records and summaries, pensions, payroll taxes—7 years

Petty cash vouchers—3 years

Property appraisals by outside appraisers—indefinitely

Property records including costs, depreciation reserves, end-of-year trial balances, depreciation schedules, blueprints and plans—indefinitely

Purchase orders (purchasing department copy)—7 years

Receiving sheets—1 year

Sales records—7 years

Scrap and salvage records (inventories, sales, etc.)—7 years

Subsidiary ledgers—7 years

Tax returns and worksheets, agents' reports, any documents relating to income tax liability—indefinitely

Time books/cards—7 years

Voucher register and schedules—7 years

Vouchers for payments to vendors, employees, etc. (including allowances and reimbursement of employees officers, etc., for travel and entertainment expenses)—7 years

W-4 forms—4 years

Workers' compensation documents—11 years

These are just guidelines for developing your own record retention policy. Apply them reasonably to minimize the risks in your individual scenarios, and ask your lawyer or accountant about how the rules may vary in your particular state, locality or industry.

Computer Files

When I was working for The Salvation Army's Western Territorial Headquarters Legal Department, they typically would generate 3000 original pieces of correspondence per year. We devised a system that worked.

Each document had a control number. January 1st the numbers began at 0000. December 31st, that year's correspondence was moved from the hard drive to floppies and stored there. The index system was the key. Here is a sample of the index system.

#	Date	To	Origin	File Folder	Active	**Destroy**
00	02/17/96	David Lake	nm	Proposal	01/01/98	01/01/99
01	06/01/96	Carl Hartness	mr	To Do	01/01/98	01/01/99
03	12/10/95		nm	Telephone Message Form	01/01/98	01/01/99

I move all my data (document) files to a ZIP disk and then have a CD made from the ZIP. That way, I can't accidentally write over the CD.

On my hard drive, there is a word processing file called INDEX. This stores all the indexes for all the years. This is like the card files that use to be in the library—a complete reference in one location.

Software

Store the software together with manuals and disks. Use shipping boxes and store them on the bookshelf. If you ever plan to use the software's technical support staff, be sure that your software is the most current (or one generation back). Frequently, tech support can't help if the software isn't the latest version.

Backing Up Software

Backing up software is something that needs to be done and should be done. But don't take the system for granted.

When we were working for a computer company that installed networks, there was a law firm that wanted to wait just a little while longer before installing a new network. Well, they waited a few days too long, the system crashed and new equipment had to be installed immediately.

The law firm was confident there would not be any problems because they had back up disks and had backed up on a regular basis. What they didn't know was that the back up equipment was also wearing out so the backed up disks were no good.

According to a recent ARMA (Association of Record Managers and Administrators) newsletter statistics indicate that nearly one third of local area networks (LAN) back up attempts fail, usually due to human error.

Set up a system for backing up the disks. Are the disks stored in a safe location? Why are the computers being backed up? Where are the disks being stored? Are they stored on site? A lot of good that would do in the case of a fire.

Have you tried to re-store it? Check out the system before it crashes. It is good practice to try re-storing a file just for the sake of learning how to do it—before a crisis.

GreenDisk
800-305-3475 http://www.greendisk.com/
To re-cycle your diskettes (4 million diskettes are discarded daily—one billion per year)

Handing Folder Tabs

One product that has been developed in the past few years is the Avery Worksheets. This product allows you to use the computer to make labels for the tabs on hanging folders. No more hand written labels—or labels that you can't see!

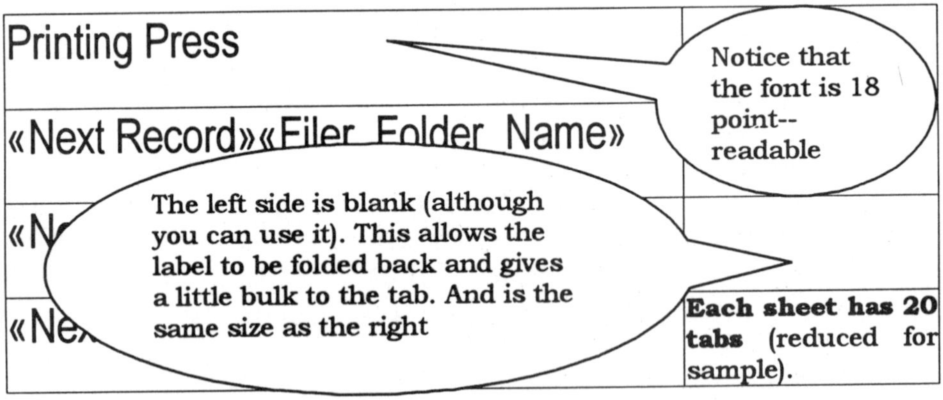

Note that the above example is a merged document. Merged documents aren't that difficult. Simply use a word processing program, create the first file (with the names of the files) as the data documents, and the second file as the template file (handing folder tab). It is possible to create even a second template for the file folder.

Equipment Combinations

Something worth considering when trying to simplify an office is to see if a piece of equipment can do multiple functions.

I posed this question to several professional speakers who typically have home-based offices and are solo operators or have a small staff. Their comments were very interesting.

Computer and internal fax modem. This combination is one of the most popular (after a telephone and answering machine). The fax and outgoing on-line service are on the same line. Pros—not a lot of time is spent on-line or faxing, convenient to print incoming faxes from printer. Great for faxing the same document to multiple people. Cons—when on-line, it is not possible to receive incoming faxes. The computer needs to be turned on in order to receive incoming faxes (even if you're not around). If there is a document that wasn't generated by the computer it is impossible to fax.

Copier, printer and fax scanner. Pros-it's very easy and not too technical. This type of technology is great to fax yourself a document then store it on the computer (remembering to toss the paper). Most printers will print labels, envelopes and postcards (assuming that labels, envelopes and postcards are laser or inkjet compatible). A copier, printer, fax, scanner was that for a limited budget this was a make-do solution. Only one laser or ink cartridge is needed.

Cons—copier had good quality for only one or two copies. Some of the copies looked too *dottie*. Remember the old dot matrix days? Many people did not use all of the functions (mostly for faxing but never scanned). Taking color printouts to a service like Kinko's was better than what the combination machine could produce. If using the printer/fax functions and the printer tray consistently had letterhead stationery in it, the faxes would also print on letterhead stationery. Outputting tended to be slow which was significantly noticeable for high volume. People using technology other than HP for printer combinations tend to have more problems.

Although these combinations of equipment are space savers if one piece goes down, the rest will also tend to be out of business.

Color Code Your Files

How many times have you sorted through mounds of paper work without finding the item you wanted? To save time, try color-coding your files. For example:

> ***Only nine percent accomplish everything they set out to do on their daily work.***
>
> ***1998 Day-Timer® Survey***

Red: anything that must be handled immediately. Green: anything that is associated with money. Blue: a high priority matter but not immediate. White: your choice

See pages 36, 50, 56 and 58 for color-coding in the home.

In an office environment, it is just as important to create a day when the office drawers will be cleaned. If possible, get as many people in the office involved as possible. Pick a time that is slow in the office or if that isn't possible come in on a Saturday or Sunday (only once—don't make it a habit).

Come to work in work clothes—no not suits and ties but jeans and sweat suits. Clothes that you don't have to worry about keeping clean, clothes that you can bend and stretch in.

Provide food. Either have treats or plan to have lunch delivered. Create a fun environment and something different for the group. Clean all the areas: desk drawers, under the desk, credenzas, bookshelves, book room files, and the storage area.

Paper for Filing	File Paper is to be Filed
5. Animal Kingdom	Animal Kingdom unless this is a subject file, the Kingdom, Animal
7. EDD	Employment Development Department
2. Linda Frazeur-Gaugert	Frazuer-Gaugert, Linda
4. IBM	IBM not International Business Machines
6. Gordon L. Miller DDS	Miller, Gordon L. DDS
1. Lorna M. Mitchell	Mitchell, Lorna M.
3. The Printing Press	Printing Press (The)

Chapter 6—Clutter Bug's Keys to Success

1. Make it easy to file.

2. File as soon as possible. The longer you wait, the bigger the job.

3. Define your needs, then select the equipment to meet that need. Select the software first (the need) and then buy the computer to run the software.

4. Protect your prime real estate. Don't overload the top of your desk, your purse or your briefcase unless you use that item several times during the day.

5. Don't file it if you don't need it. Toss it!

Clutterology

GETTING RID OF CLUTTER AND GETTING ORGANIZED!

CHAPTER 7

Test Your Filing System

Now the acid test. How did you do setting up (or re-organizing) the files?

- Are the subject names easy to remember?
- Can you find the document that you are looking for in a short period of time?
- Are the most frequently used documents nearest to you?
- Can the system expand—easily?
- Do you have a plan for documents from active to inactive, from inactive to storage, from storage to destroy?
- Why do you want or need it?
- Why is it significant?
- Is it information that I already have in another file?
- Is it timely or current?
- It is accurate and reliable?
- Can I obtain it elsewhere?
- How long do you need it?
- What would happen if it were lost?

Another Free Calendar! Put It In This Pile!

There always seems to be piles of stuff just sitting around waiting for us to get to it. So let jump into the middle of that pile!

Calendars

Many times, whether in business or for personal use, a calendar is more important than money. Getting a system that works for you will take a little time and effort. Have some fun experimenting with different styles, shapes, sizes, and those with different features. It is unlikely that the first one will be perfect. Fail your way to success.

How are you going to use the calendar? Will it go with you or stay in one place? If it is to go with you, then it must go with you. If you find that you are frequently leaving the office or the house without the calendar—look to a smaller size or larger size but something different.

52 percent of workers use calendars to keep track of their schedules, while 29 percent use organizers. Women are more likely than men to use these tools.

1998 Day-Timer® Survey

If purchasing a system and there is information that wouldn't work for you—remove it. It is not illegal, unethical or immoral to alter what the manufacturer has established. **Change your environment**. It is also possible to design your own. There are computer programs, which have fancy styles. Word processors can create a calendar by using tables with rows and columns.

Add the information that you like and need. The address section is for frequently used for names and address. My criteria for an address to go in my calendar book is, "When I am away from the office, who do I need to stay in touch with—in an emergency!" So although some of the addresses are not used for a year or two, if I am stranded in Bogota, Columbia, it is nice to have the bank's (accountant's or lawyer's) phone number.

Take the printed papers down to a copy center (Kinko's, Office Depot, Staples, etc.). Have them re-copy from one-sided to two-sided. Then have the copies bound with a comb binding. Cut it down to a personal size.

Add tabs to the calendar. If it is a big book, perhaps a tab for each quarter of the year (each month might be too much). Add a tab for the address or note section. These self-adhesive (pre-cut) tabs with inserts can be found at the stationary supply stores and are usually packaged in quantities of 25.

For all calendars, duplicate it on an occasional basis. Make sure that there is a duplicate so that if the worst thing happens (it gets lost) you don't have to re-create the whole thing. Use only one calendar.

The date book is one of the few items that I would suggest be kept almost forever. It has personal dates (graduation, christenings, etc.) as well as business meetings. The IRS has used date books to document deductions (i.e. mileage).

Mike likes the larger size. He has a three-ring notebook and his book includes a month at a glance. He doesn't have much room to write in the individual dates, but it is more important to him to see what is coming up during the month.

How much time do you have control over? If you think it's 80 percent, then schedule 80 percent of the day. At the end of the day, see how many of the scheduled activities were completed that day. If not 100 percent of the 80 percent, make the next day's schedule 70 percent. Continue this practice until you are consistently completing the tasks set out to do. It might only be one activity a day.

Tips For Using a Personal Organizer

Take it with you—always. If it's not going with you, you're not using it, and it's not working. This is supposed to be useful. What's useful to you? A place to list names and telephone number.

Day Runner® has sold 32 million organizers since 1980. About 18 million people use pre-designed organizers

Adapt—change it to fit your needs. If the organizer you purchase has sections that you have never used or haven't used in a while, take them out. Or change the tab to something you want. Under letter B list the books that people recommend or you want to read or heard about. Under R list the restaurants that you want to check out but can never remember the name. Create your own Yellow Pages.

Include or exclude birthdays. If you don't have any other location to list birthdays, the calendar is good. Because I have over 200 people's birthdays to keep track of, I input the information once on a software program (Word). I send out birthday and anniversary cards weekly (Sunday nights in front of the TV). I don't need to know that April 21 is Queen Elizabeth's birthday. The organizer has those people I would **want** to call in addition to sending a card (Mom, Dad, sisters, brothers, etc.).

Shrink to fit. Does your daughter's soccer team have a roster? Use the copy machine to reduce it to fit the organizer. Use this method for maps, forms, train/bus schedules.

Use a different color pen for each person (boss/co-workers, each child) or for each event. Keep it simple. Section off (left/right or top/bottom) the day (if there is room) to indicate work/home; husband/wife; or adults/children.

As a family, meet once a week to coordinate, talk and add dates to the schedule. The Royal family sits down every six months to plan for the next six months and beyond. For Diana, she waited until she received the schedule from the school with Prince William and Prince Harry's vacation days, school plays, and special events, and then she (and the Prince of Wales) would schedule their business around those dates.

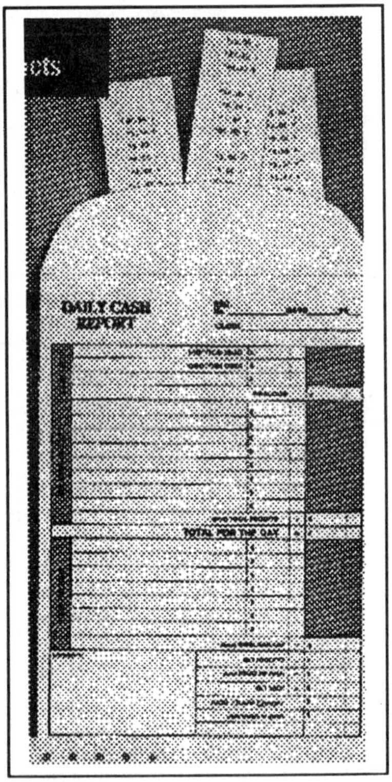

Keep an envelope for receipts. No need to put the receipts in pockets, billfold or the closest spot.

Get the credit card (or business card) holder for the organizer, even if you are not planning to keep your credit cards or other peoples' business cards in the organizer. Instead, include your business cards. Have two or three in each place. Carry one or two of your spouse's or other associates if you frequently find yourself saying, "You should contact..."

Planning a vacation or remodeling the living room? Use (or make) a section in the organizer.

Are you a service-based business with clients? Keep a section for each client. Include notes, phone calls, ideas, action plans, deadlines, etc.

Create a special section for Christmas gift giving. Then during the year if you have an idea for Christmas, jot it down or if you buy a present, list it in this section.

Have children? Create a section for each child including clothes sizes and preferences or wants.

Monthly, Weekly or Daily—what is better? Monthly is an overview and gives a good snap shot of what's coming up. Weekly is good if there are more details to attend to. Daily is for scheduling hour per hour in addition to a To Do list, Calls to Make, etc.

Whenever possible, write it down. Don't try to remember the things that you need to do. Keep your mind free for other tasks rather than trying to remember.

If plans are to use an electronic calendar, consider these features:

1. How easily does the software allow you to rescheduling appointments? Do you have to delete the old entry and retype the whole new entry? Or do you just have to change the date?

2. Does it have a day, week or month viewing ability? Sometimes it is easier to view each day totally, but much quicker to find an activity when viewing the whole month.

3. Does the layout have the information you need?

4. Many calendars have a section for activities (to do list). If the activity is not completed today, does the software automatically carry forward the uncompleted task to the next day (which is called creeping) or do you have to re-type everything?

5. Does the calendaring software have word processing ability? Features like auto correct, spell checkers, templates, fonts, margins and other things that we take for granted these days might not be in the calendar software.

6. How many entries per day will it hold? If trying to schedule 5-10 appointments per day, will the software support it?

7. Does the software have auto dial (the phone will dial the phone number for you—no more wrong numbers) or alarms to notify you of an appointment or activity?

8. What does the printout look like? Because my calendars are small pocket size, frequently the information that I included for the appointment (name, telephone number, address, contact person, and directions) didn't appear on the page because it was too small.

EZ Pocket
$27.95 plus $4.95 shipping and handling.
PO Box 2328
Basalt CO 81621
800-681-8681 xws.com/ezpocket ezpocket@compuseve.com
EZ Pocket is a monthly calendar that hangs on the back of a door (or on the wall). Also available is a *week at a glance* which with a pocket for Monday, Tuesday, Wednesday, Thursday, Friday with pockets large enough to store legal size folders. $27.95 plus $4.95 shipping and handling. This system can be adapted for use for projects (Girls Scouts, Church, Budget, etc.).

1/3 of American never plan their daily work.
78% of the workforce list getting more exercise as a goal.
65% of the workforce would like to spend more time with family
52% of workers use calendars to keep track of their schedules.
29% use organizers.
33% have written career goals.

Tickler Systems/Future File/Suspense Files

There are several types of tickler systems. The most common have 43 hanging files, which are labeled 1-31 and Jan-Dec.

Place in the appropriate month, those papers for you to follow-up on. At the beginning of each day, review that day's folder. At the beginning of each new month, sort contents into the appropriate days.

Some variations on the tickler file are:

- 1st week, 2nd week, 3rd week, 4th week, 5th week
- 1st-7th; 8th-14th; 15th-21st; 21-EOM (end of month)
- Jan/Feb/Mar; Apr/May/Jun; Jul/Aug/Sep; and Oct/Nov/Dec

The benefits to tickler systems are:

- Everything is there for that date. If you're looking for your airline tickets or theatre tickets for the March 15th event, there they are.

- It is not necessary to keep touching the document or to create a file for just one and/or two pieces of papers.

The disadvantages to a tickler system:

- You know that airline ticket is in there somewhere—but where?

- Don't remember you were we to follow up in ten days or two months? So many folders to look through that it would almost be easier just to pile them on top of the desk.

- You forget to look in there on a daily basis, and that important event has not been posted. Create a reason to look in the folder that would motivate you—a daily cartoon, money randomly drop into folders, etc.

Reading File

Many of us have materials that need to be read as part of our position. Have one location for reading. Then when time is available, read the material. If finding time is difficult, find a quiet place (break-room, the lobby or even the company library) and read on a regular basis. Even if it is 10-30 minutes a day, over time, progress is made.

If the pile for reading is falling over, are there one or two items that are larger than the others are? Read that first. If magazines are being held to read just one article, rip or photocopy the article.

Set limits. How long should the material be kept so that the material is current and up-to-date?

On-Going Paper Work

I have a system of using plastic project folders for my papers. Whenever I get more than one piece of paper on one subject or the paper size is smaller than 8½x11, I slip it into the folder. These folders are available through Century Plastic (see page 28).

This system works for me. However, there are pros and cons:

Pros:

1. When looking for a piece of paper (or pieces of paper) it is easier and quicker to sort through the folder than each and every single piece of paper.

2. I re-use the folders.

3. They don't require labeling and since the front is clear plastic, I can see immediately what the top piece of paper is.

4. There are several different colors of backs to choose from (red, green, and blue) so that if I wanted to, the color could have significance.

5. I file the folders by broad categories (To Doing) and place them in a hanging file folder in the desk drawer.

Cons:

1. The plastic is slick and sometimes when I'm looking for a piece of paper and I am using my lap, everything slides off!

2. If I pile rather than file, the pile is slick and everything in the pile slides all over the desk and onto the floor.

3. As there are no tabs or file cuts, I have to expose the full front (or as much as necessary) before I recognize what it is.

4. Plastic doesn't stand up by itself too well. Too few projects in a hanging file might cause all files to slide down and start curling. (I wish I had this problem—only a few projects. However, when the projects start to slide down, I move them to a smaller box bottom or standard file to compensate. I am also using cardboard stiffeners—the ones from the dry cleaners that come with Mike's folded dress shirts—so they stand up a little easier.

Magazines

Set up a circulation list to circulate magazines in the office. It might be necessary to have a separate list for each magazine, set of minutes or reports that your office/department receives. Or create a form with all individual names on it and photo copy it.

Set a limit on how long each person will be loaned the magazine. This eliminates the **black hole** individuals—things go in but never come out. (A variation on the use it or lose it principal.)

After circulation has been completed, store the material. This way, if an individual didn't finish reading a particular issue, there is the opportunity to finish reading it.

Magazine	***Who To***	***$***	***Renewed***	***Retention***
Inside Network	MFR	99.	09/97	Two back copies
Sharing Ideas	MFR NKM	39.	07/97	0

If you're planning to keep the magazine and the magazine doesn't already provide one, create an index of the articles (include volume, issue, month and page). If this information is on computer then use the power of the computer to search for information rather than trying to search for the information by hand.

Minutes

Create an index for your meeting minutes. That way when an item starts to be rehashed, referring back to the previous minutes might help the current discussion.

Putting Out Fires

Do you find yourself putting out fires? If so, these are messages that systems are out of control or not in place. Take a close look at these areas and design systems to control them.

Why did it occur? What can be done to prevent its reoccurrence? If it does reoccur, how can I (we) handle it better next time?

Telephones

Telephones are a part of our lives, and sometimes it feels like they are a part of our bodies.

5 percent of American commuters use their cellular phone during commuting.

1998 Day-Timer® Survey

Where you work (and where you live), are there enough phones? Are you frequently running to the phone? If so, have another phone installed where you frequently are. We had one put in our garage. Seems like just as we are going or coming, the phone rings and it's up a flight of stairs to the nearest phone. (See page 87.)

By each phone have a pen and some paper. Try the same trick here with pens as on your desk. Only have one. People are not dumb, if there is only one pen; they tend to leave it.

If your office is small and the person sending you information is sending a cover sheet also, it's a waste of paper. 3M (www.3m.com/post-it) has the little Post-It® Notes for faxes or just write the information on the paper. It works.

If you are working on a project but keep getting interrupted by the telephone, let the answering machine or voice mail pick up the call. Nothing says that you have to answer the phone, even when you are there!

Would the phone be more effective if it were mounted on the wall or a longer cord was added on or perhaps even mounted on the side of the desk?

A tip on storing telephone books. In the larger metropolitan areas, the phone books are huge. If they are placed on a bookshelf, they tend to slide down. Store the phone book with the spine to the back of the shelf. They stay up a little longer!

This tip was from a student in my class: pull out the rail from a hanging file. Put the rail in the phone book as close to the spine as possible. Hang the phone book in the files.

Design your own telephone message forms. It's easy to do.

I was always taking messages for Mike, so I designed one just for him.

Telephone Message for Mike ~~Rounds~~

Date: ______________________ Time: _________

Mr./Ms: ___________________________________

Student: C CL H I M N PM PO S W Bureau

These are the codes for our classes—which we know.

Company: _________________________________

Phone Number: ____________________________

Alternative Number: ________________________

❐ Returned your call. ❐ Please call back.

❐ Will call again. Message:

0398 (see page 100)

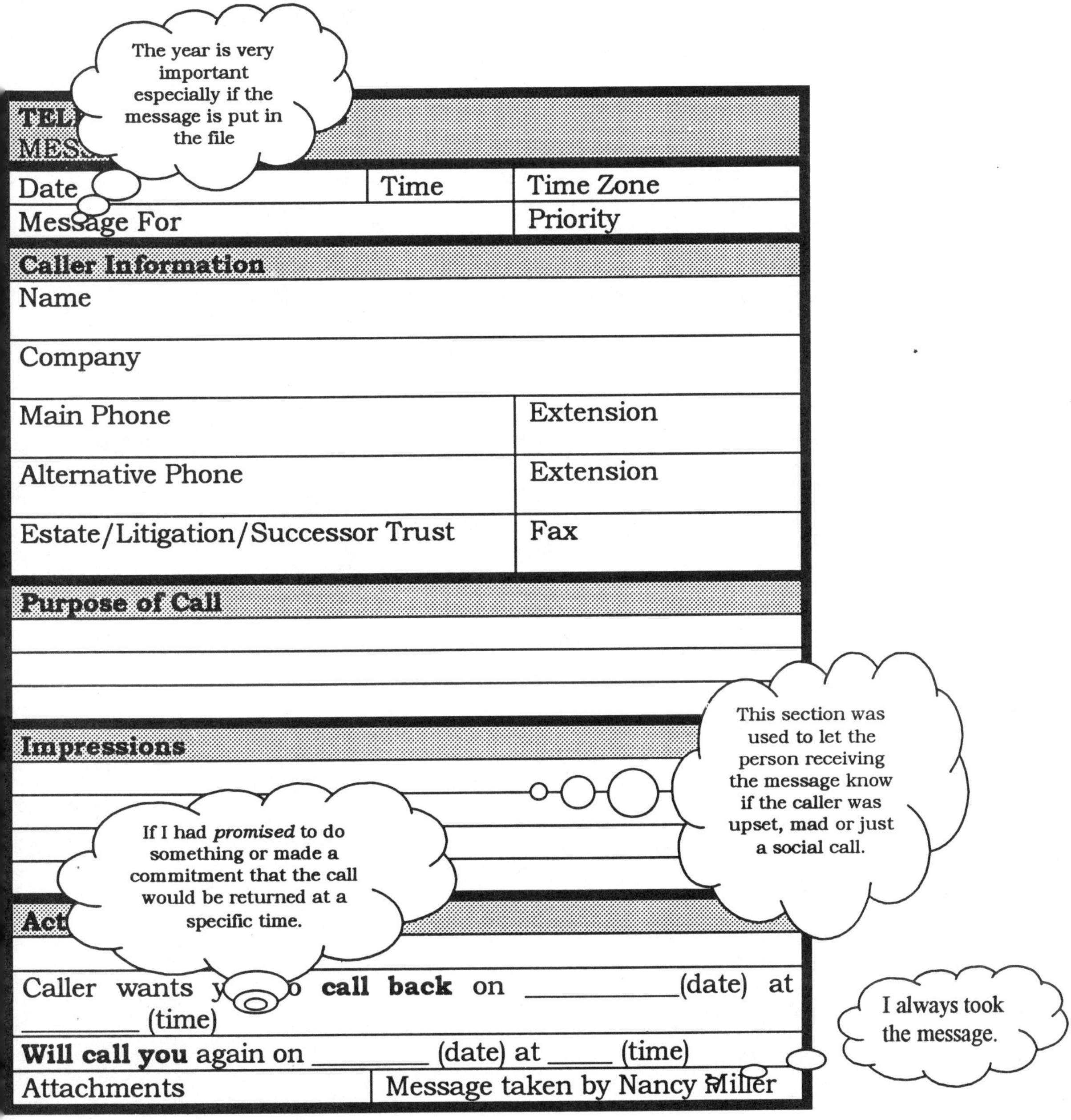

This message pad was 8½x11.

Finally, if you think you have it bad—although the Queen of England does not have an in box, she has what are called the *red boxes.* These red boxes are leather boxes with her initials on it. Several times during the day, a servant (office worker) brings in her boxes, which are fastened shut. In the boxes are government documents, etc. But, these boxes keep coming every day, Monday to Sunday, and even when she is on vacation or out of the office.

Chapter 7—Clutter Bug's Keys to Success

1. Change the calendar or date book to work for you.
2. If your papers are date oriented, consider setting up a tickler system.
3. Set a limit to your reading file. Read within 30 days or toss!
4. Use the telephone as a tool. Telephones don't rule our lives!
5. Design forms to work for you.

Clutterology

GETTING RID OF CLUTTER AND GETTING ORGANIZED!

CHAPTER 8

BOB SIMPLIFIES HIS LIFE:
I TOOK ALL OF MY WORLDLY POSESSIONS TO OUR LOCAL SCRAP-YARD, AND THEY COMPACTED EVERYTHING INTO A SINGLE, ONE-CUBIC-YARD, VERY LOW-MAINTENANCE PLANT STAND.
YOU SHOULD SEE WHAT IT DOES WHEN I PLUG IT IN!

Don't Throw That Away—It Fits Something—I Just Can't Remember What!

There are several areas that have special consideration because of the nature of the collection.

Books

Why do you want to keep them?

- Entertainment—then keep them for as long as you are re-reading them.
- Reference—be sure that you update your reference books on a regular bases (dictionaries every 10 years). Do they actually get referred to? If not, they're book-ends.
- Work related—these aren't necessarily for reading but to keep you up-to-date on the industry.

Books are a source and resource for many people. Store all of your books together.

Look at the copyright date. If the date is more than five years old, ask yourself if the subject matter has changed since then. If yes, get rid of the book.

Could you give the book to your local library, charity or sell them to a used bookstore? Used bookstores will buy books. Look in the Yellow Pages under Bookstore-Used. Call the bookstore to see if they are interested in purchasing your books. Bookstores have different *themes* or particular areas of interest. In some areas, the used bookstores have developed a list other used bookstores in the area.

You won't get a lot of money for the books, but it does add up and it gives you a chance to go out for dinner one night. If you want to exchange the money for in-store credit, there is a slightly higher value.

Reduce the number of books that you have. Keep your favorites. Instead of 300 books, reduce the number down to a shelf full of books.

Women are more likely than men to read during free time.

1998 Day-Timer® Survey

My minister did something that I thought was crazy at the time, but now seemed very wise. He gave away **all** of his books on a regular basis every five years. This would be an advance clutterologist. However, he recognized the benefit of giving.

Use the public library. They have all the new novels, they will put books on reserve, and it is possible in many libraries to re-new the books by phone.

Talk to your local library regarding donations. Each library has different collections. Here are some general guidelines for donating books to the libraries:

1. If the books (and/or magazines) have been stored in the garage for over six months, have bugs, mites, spiders or are smelly, the library does not want them.

2. Ask for a receipt from the library and the donation can be used by you as a taxable contribution on your income taxes.

3. Call the local libraries (yes, more than one) and find out what type of books they are looking for: English, grammar, science, technology, social science, business, sports, arts, photography, or literature. Match your books with their needs.

4. Frequently libraries will post a **Most Wanted** list. This is a list of the best sellers that they are interested in. If you frequently buy best sellers or are trying to decide on what best seller to buy, check the list, buy the book, read the book, then donate it to the library. Typically these types of books go immediately into general circulation (are cataloged and put on the shelf for patrons).

5. Are you subscribing to *People* magazine? Read the magazine and then donate it (immediately) to the library. The library may only have enough funds for one subscription to a popular magazine and will appreciate the contribution. Did you know that you could cancel your subscription at any time? The company will send you a refund for the unused portion of the subscription. Be sure to ask that they send you a refund. I came across one company that unless the subscriber specifically asked for the refund, they kept the money!

6. Our local library has a book drop (looks like a drive up United States Postal Service mailbox) for returning books and one for donating books. We don't even have to get out of our car!

7. The donation of books which are sold at 10¢ to 25¢ go towards items which can't be purchased with county (state or whatever issuing authority) money—like food or goodies when there is a presenter, performer, book reading, etc.

8. Back issues of any magazine are accepted. There is no general time frame but be sure that the magazines, like the books, don't have bugs in them.

9. Are you an avid romance reader? So are other people. If you are donating your romances to the same library, check with the library to see if they have room for the romances or have they started to sell the novels. Perhaps switch (or alternate) between two or more libraries.

Ask the library if they have a **subscription donation form**. The form includes the date, your name, address, telephone number and magazine title. In addition to books, libraries also frequently look for donations of records (yes, those things before tapes and CDs), videotapes and audiotapes.

The Care of Fine Books
by Jare Greenfield
Price: $19.95 224 pages
ISBN: 1558210032

Car

Keeping the car clean can be difficult. We have two little trash cans in each car. One is just too small but the two bins lock each other in instead of falling over.

On a regular basis, empty the trash. Most shopping centers, parking structures, convenience stores and even some drive-thrus have trash receptacles. We have also placed a trash container in the garage, that way we don't have to drag the trash all the way in the house.

If you find that you have a lot of trash in your car but you're not getting it out of the car quickly put a large (or as big as physically possible) trash can by the car so it is easy to empty. The kind you would buy for the bathroom. Don't go to the auto places—you'll just get more of the same—the ones that don't work. Or if you park outside, put trash liners in the car and then pick up the trash.

Whenever I am in the car waiting for a few minutes, I take the time to sort through the stuff in the car.

One year, Mike and I were on a road show to Northern California teaching classes in the evening. I emptied the contents of the interior of the car into a bag and took it into the hotel. I dumped the stuff on the bed and sorted. It was amazing what was in the car.

Map book—in most large metropolitan areas, a separate map book is needed. It is useful to keep this book where you can reach it **when you need it** and that it is in working order.

Because we have two cars, his car has the most recent map book. Every other year I purchase a new map book and put it in his car. Then his old book goes in my car. My old book is donated.

What do you need in your car? One thing that I was constantly looking for was paper and pen. We had a scratch pad but it didn't fit in the center console. I went down to my local quick printer and asked that the pad be trimmed to XxY. Now, the paper fits into the console.

The ashtray is used for more than ashes. When I belonged to several organizations and they each required their own nametag, I put the nametags in the ashtray. If I remembered, I would put it on during the drive to the meeting or if I forgot, I could go back out to the parking lot to get it.

Growing up and learning to drive in Minnesota, I started a system that I still use today. In Minnesota, in the fall and spring, the tires needed to be changed from/to snow tires. It was at that time, when I had the mechanics look over the car and take care of the problems before they happened. Now, what I tell them, "I don't want to see you for a year."

In Los Angeles (a place without snow tires), I use the yearly renewal tags to act as the cue to fix the car. I still take it to the dealership yearly. With computers, they know what was done previously and what should be done now based on mileage and I add what I have noticed while driving.

After the dealership, I take the car to the car wash. I have the car's interior, engine and exterior given the royal treatment.

If you have a garage door opener in your car and are constantly fumbling to find it, Velcro® the garage door opener to the sun visor. It always stays in place and is easy to find.

Look in your Yellow Pages telephone book to find a hazardous waste disposal unit in your area for disposal of paint, motor oil, motor fluids, medicines, antifreeze, pesticides and car batteries. Many organizations provide this service free of charge.

Collections

Museums are always upgrading their collections and only display the best. With our collection, we should also be upgrading and displaying the best of the collection. Mere quantity is not enough. Is there a way to reduce the collection?

What about that matchbook collection? What is the purpose of the collection? To say or prove that we have been in those places? Or is it in case the lights go out for a very long time? Perhaps you should reduce the collection to a memorable few.

What shape is the stamp collection in? Why are we keeping the collection—because of its value when it is sold? Sell it. Remember the saying—what you own, owns you. Is the collection creating pleasure or has it become work?

An idea that might work for some is to frame the collection. I have framed Mike's service career, which includes his discharge papers, plus several medals that Mike is particularly pleased with. We also framed his professional drumming career. It turned into a fun project, working with the framer and trying to get the drumsticks framed.

When considering framing a collection, select items that are representative of the collection. Also, keep an eye out for continuity or theme or color. When selecting a framer, ask if they do preservation (acid-free matting, not cutting/altering the document).

When you get the frame back, display it with honor.

Sotheby's Caring For Antique's A Guide To Handling, Cleaning, Display and Restoration
by Mette Tang Simpson and Michael Huntley
Price: $24.95
Paperback
ISBN: 185029867X

Day-Light Savings Time

Do you need to reset the time on the microwave but can't remember how to do it and haven't gotten around to finding the owner's manual? Get index cards (or maybe a Post-It® Note) write the directions on the paper and put it under the appliance (microwave) or tape it to the bottom (telephone) or tape it (with a Post It Glue Stick) to the side of the unit or on the wall.

Garage

For many people, the garage is either where the automobile is parked or it's the storage unit.

Look around the garage. What is being used on a regular basis and what can be tossed out? The garage is one area where we must be conscious of toxic and hazardous chemicals.

Pick a corner of the garage and just take a visual inventory of the contents in the garage. Can shelves be added in the garage to add more space? Can the rafters be used in some fashion?

If there is oil on the floor, check out the local hardware store. There are solvents that will clean up the floor. Paint the walls white to make it look clean. We had the garage floor treated with an anti-slip paint so that when the floor is wet (after washing or during rain) that the crutches and I don't have intimate relations with the floor!

Hobbies—Knitting, Sewing and Crafts

Hobbies are fun and are meant to be enjoyed and reduce stress. Frequently, stress is produced when either the hobby starts to grow and take over our life or we are no longer active in the hobby.

When I started to collect books and magazines on the British Royal Family, I limited the size of the collection to my office. I could collect as much as I wanted to, but it had to stay within the four walls. The day came when I sold the collection. It was time, it was no longer fun. Now that I am cutting back, I am saving only the couple of books that I frequently reference. I enjoy it.

If the hobby is a project (a jigsaw puzzle, remodeling the bathroom), when the job is completed, put away the toys (the tables, the tools, the stuff). Perhaps throw away that half-empty tube of glue. If you didn't like it a lot in the first place, in ten years (when you get around to your next project) you might have forgotten how difficult it was to work with.

To reduce the size of your collection, take pictures of it or take a small portion of it. A quilt that was your great-grandmothers and is now worn out, can be made into a doll blanket.

Crafts and Hobbies
by Reader's Digest Staff
Price: $24.95 Hardcover
456 pages
ISBN: 0895770636
Included is every conceivable craft for anyone to learn.

Quilt Restoration: A Practical Guide
by Camille Dalphand Cognac
Price: $29.95 Hardcover
ISBN: 0939009838

Keys

How many keys are you carrying around? Do you need them all on a regular basis? Do you know what they are for?

I can't remember what every key is for and sometimes describing it is difficult. The easy way is to take a picture of the object (the car, the file cabinet, or the desk) and tape the key to the back of the picture.

Those cute little key rings usually take up more space than is practical. A house key, car key and office key are probably the most used keys. Have a separate key ring for the other keys. Many house entry locks are now number pads instead of a lock and key.

Store the key in the keyhole of that object (in the suitcase, in the desk, in the file cabinet). If the object is metal, use a hide-a-key on the backside of the unit.

Check with the dealership about having a second key made. More and more keys have electronic parts, special designs that are not easily duplicated. Include the key code in the organizer.

Also check with AAA. They frequently have a service to duplicate your key at a low fee as part of the membership.

Light Bulbs

If you can't remember which light bulb for which fixture and wattage you need:

- Take pictures of the lamps, chandelier, and halogen lamps.
- Write on the back of the picture the buying instructions (where you found it, when you purchased it, etc.)
- Or when you buy the bulbs, staple the pictures to the wrapper.

- Include tips and tricks for replacing.

Does your clock or watch need a new battery. Use the same system as the light bulbs.

Luggage

There is some pretty spectacular luggage that is on the market now. But do we have a couple of pieces sitting in the closet or in the garage?

Pull all the pieces of luggage out and take a close look at it in the light of day.

First, does the luggage meet your needs? Is there something that you just hate about that piece? If so, get rid of it.

Does the piece have a key? Can the key be found? Don't worry, sometimes a key can be made from the local locksmith. There are straps and locks that can be attached around the outside of the suitcase.

If there is a key for the suitcase, instead of leaving the key on your key ring, take a safety pin and slip the key through the safety pin and attach it to the inside of the suitcase, using it's lining.

If there is a possibility that somehow the suitcase could get locked with the key(s) in the suitcase, take a rubberband and loop it through the hole of the key and attach the key to the handle.

When we travel, we have a collapsible bag that we line the bottom of the suitcase with. We use it for dirty clothes or an extra bag on the way home.

Three major airlines (United, Delta and Southwest) will be limiting the number of carry-on bags. The rules apply to all classes of service and all flights. Laptop, bags with duty-free merchandise are included as an item of carry-on. Exceptions are: small purses (men's or women's), food for eating on board and aides for the disabled, coats, child seat, camera.

On crowded flights Southwest allows just one carry-on item as does Northwest Airlines on all flights (except laptops, briefcase or purse).

Pets and Animals

Although pets bring a great deal of pleasure to people, they also come with their own stuff. Again, collect all the pet stuff together and see what the total looks like.

Are there any objects that the pet doesn't like (food or toys)? Get rid of them or give them to the pet shelter.

Is all of this stuff necessary? Reduce and simplify. Clean up the blanket or pillow the animal sleeps on.

The pet-repellent sprays to keep pets off living-room couches or beds do work—maybe. Many of these sprays contain chemicals that can cause skin and eye irritation if you, your family or your pet is exposed to **freshly** sprayed surfaces.

I found a pet supply organizer and travel tote: The Pet Pockets it is a unique organizer for pet accessories. There are 11 pockets of various sizes (front and back) for such things as grooming supplies, toys, veterinary records, collars, leashes, treats, etc.

Together Enterprises
11905 124th Ave NE
Kirkland WA 98034
800-746-9604; 206-823-4604 fax
Price: $16.95.

Plants

Plants add beauty to the world. However, they do take work—not as much work as a pet. Take a close look at the plant. Is it alive? Can it be fixed? If so, fix it. Many of the local garden centers and some of the super hardware stores now provide help and care.

What about the pots and the dirt? If there are no plants, get rid of the accessories. If you are not going to be planting for a while, how long will it be before you get back to it? A year or two? Calculate the storage cost, energy cost and replacement cost for those two years. Would it be cheaper to replace it in two years?

Take out all of the bud vases and single vases. How many of them do we need? Frequently, offices will have a collection of vases. No one knows where they came from or who they belong to, but they stay. Even in a good year, the husband only brings home flowers one occasion at a time.

Photographs

Do you look at photographs and ask yourself who was this? When was this taken?

Since high school, I have written on the back of photographs who, what, where, when, how, and by whom. Who is this picture of (what is their age when the picture was taken), what is the event, activity, where were they (full address and ZIP code if possible) and who took the picture? I try to identify each person in the picture and indicate by a question mark those that I have no clue.

A little at a time, this is easy. Catching up will require some time, but start now.

Did you know that unexposed film can last up to six months past its expiration date—if it was stored in its original container in a cool, dry place. one year past it expiration date if stored in the refrigerator. A roll of film, once in the camera should be used within one month.

Do you need the negatives? Reprints can be made from the original picture. Take a look at the pictures. Even if it was free, do you need (or want) two of each print? Are some pictures not what you wanted? If so, toss them out immediately–the total black or total white shots aren't very picturesque.

Recently, I had pictures from Christmas that I wanted to share with my family. Instead of getting reprints, I went down to Kinko's™ and had color copies made of the pictures (5 to a page or something like that). It was a way to share with my family.

Something to watch out for is if the paper and products are acid-free. Without acid-free products, what is being stored may have a shorter life.

Exposures
2800 Hoover Road
Stevens Point WI 54481
800-222-4947

Creative Memories
2815 Clearwater Rd
St. Cloud MN 56302-1839
800-468-9335
Use creative scrapbook albums to preserve photos, stories and memorabilia. Creative Memories offers in-home educational classes for private gatherings of friends and family.

Creating Keepsakes Scrapbook Magazine
354 Mountain Way Dr
Orem UT 84058
801-352-0517
$19.97 per year for six issues

An Ounce of Preservation: A Guide To The Care of Paper and Photographs
by Craig A. Tuttle
Price: $12.95 Paperback 111 pages
ISBN: 1569250215

Century Photo Products (see page 28).

Sports

Another area that creates a lot of clutter is sports and its' equipment. In the past few years, there have been a number of gadgets to organize sports equipment.

Before organizing the equipment, we need to ask the appropriate individual or ourselves if it is still necessary to keep the equipment. Does the activity still bring pleasure or does just the site of that expensive equipment bring anguish?

There are more and more second-hand stores for used sports equipment. Check them out and see if you can sell them the equipment. Some of the stores might work on a consignment basis—they put the equipment on the floor, and when (if) it is sold, the store takes its' commission and you get the rest.

Vacations

The American workforce is twice as likely to take a 1-3 day trip than a long vacation.

1998 Day-Timer® Survey

Before leaving on vacation, set a limit as to what you are bringing back. Is it going to be a thousand postcards or just one nice souvenir (a piece of jewelry or a decoration for the house)? It is possible to buy something that you know will break. If it breaks before getting home, get rid of it.

Or take pictures on vacation instead of making purchases. The pictures are personal and of sites that you saw. Postcards are also nice. Whenever we travel, whether it be a vacation or just traveling out of town, I get a postcard and send it to my mom.

She kept a number of them and gave them back to me recently. It was neat. Not a lot could be said on the postcard so it was mainly the highlights. I had forgotten most of the places we had been. Why not send yourself postcards from wherever you are?

Before going home, at the last packing, look at what you are packing and decide if you want it. There might be papers, maps, directions and other types of material that doesn't need to go home. *The trash can is our friend.*

Videotapes and Audiotapes

Use a computer system to index and list the audiotapes and videotapes in a database. There are some computer software programs that are only a few dollars (under $20) that could work well for you. Develop an indexing system (categories) to list the tapes. Even a word processing program can work.

When talking with Dave Morton, President of Sound Choice, an audio and video duplicating company, his recommendations for storage and increasing the life of the tape are:

1. Keep the tapes airtight. For example, if the tapes are in a cardboard box, tape the seams of the box reducing the amount of air into the box.

2. Keep the tapes as dry as possible.

3. Keep the temperature under 100 degrees and as consistent as possible. Store in a dry cool location.

4. The media starts breaking down between five to seven years. However, there are no standards within the industry. It has been know that tapes last as long as 10-12 years. That means, sooner or later, you (or someone else) will have to transfer the tapes that you now have to another media (possibly to CDs).

Audiotapes can be used for many other things. For instance, if you frequently travel and miss your child's bedtime, read a story into a tape so that at bedtime, the child can still hear your voice and have a story.

ECO Media
5427 East La Palma Avenue
Anaheim CA 92807
800-359-4601
They re-cycle videotapes

Prince Charles, when he was younger, and his two baby brothers were royal pains; so he created a story about Scotland to entertain his brothers. They enjoyed his story so much that Prince Charles turned the story into a book (AISN: 0374356130) and then into a videotape (ISBN: 6302287677) and it now sells worldwide.

What other use can you find for audiotapes? How about directions? Directions to your house, directions to the kids what to do when they get home from school, directions on how to do a specific task (step 1, take the clothes out of the dryer; step 2, put them in the clothes basket; step 3 take the basket to your room; step 4 fold the clothes; step 5 put clothes away; step 6 put the clothes basket back in the laundry room).

When the tape starts to whine—time to get rid of it! If the tape (look at the black stuff) is shiny, it is beginning to wear out. Look at the felt piece under the tape. What type of condition is that in? The worse for wear, the more likely the tape is not in good condition.

You can sell audiotapes to record stores. Look in the telephone book or I found several on the Internet with GTE Big Book under the category records—used.

What they look for is:

1. The more recent the better. Like yesterday.

2. All original—the box, the original j-card (that is the paper that slips into the cassette box).

3. Unbroken tapes.

4. Tapes in good condition.

5. Different locations have different criteria. The artist, the title, the condition plus how much inventory they have at the time.

6. The going rate per tape is between 25¢ and $1.25.

Chapter 8—Clutter Bug's Keys to Success

1. Find items that will work for you. Don't go shopping in the auto department for help in your car. Perhaps shop in the bathroom department—get creative.

2. If you were to die, would your heirs know what was important to you, what you wanted to give to whom and where to find important documents?

3. Write (or tape—audio/video) yourself instructions to activities.

4. Complete the project. Put it **all** away!

5. Anything unidentifiable, toss.

6. Audiotapes and videotapes will deteriorate over time. Store properly to increase life and transfer to new media when required.

Clutterology

GETTING RID OF CLUTTER AND GETTING ORGANIZED!

CHAPTER 9

VELEY

Who's Turn Is It To Keep The Fruitcake This Year?

I was born on Christmas Day—my mother said that I was wrapped in Christmas colors—red hair and green eyes. To add to my excitement, my husband and I got married two days after Christmas.

Christmas adds to the excitement and stress of *normal, everyday* life. The holidays come with added clutter.

What surprised me about Christmas (and entertaining in general) was that the first year (time) it was nearly a disaster—it wasn't as eloquent as Aunt Audrey's, the Christmas wrappings wasn't as stunning as Rita's, and there weren't as many people as Mom had over. However, year after year, Christmas got better. Through trial and error, I had to learn what worked and what didn't. What worked for other family members didn't work as well for me.

Cards and Lists

For some, Christmas cards become a tedious and expensive activity.

If you are computerized, there are some programs that are simple (and inexpensive) and can help you organize your list. If not, there are a variety of manual systems. Use an index card which lists the person's name on top and then the address. Or purchase an address book used exclusively for a Christmas list.

Take a look at why you are sending Christmas cards. Do you like sending out Christmas cards? If not, why are you doing it?

I have a simple system for *weeding out* the names on the Christmas card list. We keep track of the people we send to and who we receive cards/letters from. If we don't receive a reply from someone for two years, we remove him or her from the list. The logic behind the two years is that sometimes, people have a bad year and might not get around to sending out cards that year. Perhaps we should try the *three strikes* rule!

The Royal family has a code for events that the Queen invites them to—MOTA (morally obligated to attend). There are a few people on the Christmas list that I continue to send even if they haven't reciprocated—MOTS (morally obligated to send) like a brother, a brother-in-law, and aunt or uncle.

Do you need to send out Christmas cards every year? No, it doesn't have to be yearly. One year, we didn't send out Christmas cards and only a couple of people actually mentioned that they missed our letter. Well, it was a little more than a few. People enjoyed our letter.

Many people are now sending out Christmas letters in addition to Christmas cards. From my point of view, I enjoy the letters more than the cards. We were doubling our expense by sending a letter with the card. We no longer send out the cards. Talking to others, they like the cards and hate the letter.

We are trying out a new concept. We are having Christmas postcards designed. We can have a 4-color postcard designed and printed for less than purchasing store-bought Christmas cards. 500 postcards for $95 plus $100 for the graphic work!

Last year, my husband and I talked about the Christmas cards that we received. We don't decorate the house with them; we just put them in a basket. We decided that after I opened the card, doubled checked the address and check received on this Christmas list, I gave them to my husband. After he enjoyed the card/letter, he tossed out the card.

Although this sounds heartless, this was actually very effective (and his idea) and a way of simplifying. We discussed where the pleasure of the Christmas card was (in getting the card, hearing from family and friends).

Many people read Christmas cards after Christmas as a way of wrapping up the season. It is during an unhurried time and it is possible to reflect and enjoy.

The Queen and her husband, the Duke of Edinburgh started to personally sign Christmas cards around August. They sign only a few at a time (because the Duke has very bad arthritis) when they have a moment (on the plane, on the train, etc.)

St. Jude's Ranch for Children
100 St. Jude St
Box 985
Boulder City NV 89005
702-294-7100; 800-492-3562; 702-294-7171 fax
Accepts the fronts of Christmas cards and other greeting cards and uses the pictures to decorate new cards, which it sells as nonprofit fund raising.

Paper—Ribbons, Paper and Boxes

I remember when growing up, my mother, sisters, and aunts saving Christmas paper (or birthday, etc.) that they liked. Learning from them, when I moved from apartment to apartment—state to state, I moved empty boxes and had a special drawer just for boxes and paper.

I finally asked myself why was I saving all of these boxes and papers. If I never bought another wrapping paper or a box, I would have enough until the year 2020.

57% of us save pretty gift paper to re-use.

Reused vs. new—if you plan to reuse, don't buy any new paper, use up what you have first (that's why you are reusing it). If you find that you just can't reuse the paper, then toss all the old and buy new. Don't buy any new paper until **all** the wrapping paper is gone.

My sister, Rita, has always had the most remarkable, memorable and interesting wrapping paper that I have ever seen. She spent a great deal of time, money and energy on the wrapping paper itself.

This past Christmas, I overheard Rita saying that this would be the last year for the fancy wrapping paper. For years it gave her pleasure (I also think that it was also an expression of her artistic talents). However, now, it's not as much fun for her and her traditions have changed.

If you find that you are running short on time and the Christmas presents still aren't wrapped, hire someone to do it. Many department stores or shipping stores provides this service. Or hire a student. I remember my father always brought his presents to me to wrap. He taped the boxes and wrote who they were to. All I had to do was wrap them. I loved wrapping the presents—it was fun. Also, to save yourself from the feeling of overwhelm (wrapping all the presents the night before) wrap each gift as you purchase it!

Decorating

When I was in college, I would get a tree, but had trouble decorating it. So, I started to invite my friends over to help me decorate the tree. The tree decorating party was fun and people began to look forward to it. When I got married, we continued the tradition. Then we had too many people over, so we now have a yearly Christmas party.

Do you have a set of Christmas china that you enjoy? Why not set the table and keep it set throughout the season. What a lovely decoration.

I heard of an old custom, which said that the table was always set and had an extra plate. That way, if an unexpected guest arrived at dinnertime, they would be welcomed to the family table—because they were expected. Also if good luck showed up at your doorstep, the family was always ready to receive it! I don't know how true it is or if that was the custom, but we do enjoy our china on the table all season long—just like the department stores.

Gifts and Stuff

Gifts seem to add another dimension of clutter. In addition to the *real* clutter of gifts, there is also the *emotional* clutter of gifts.

When we give gifts, we try to give things that won't stay around for very long—plants, balloons, food or tickets.

Whenever we have a birthday or Christmas party, we ask that people don't bring gifts. Occasionally, we will ask that they bring an unopened gift for a child and then we take it to the Children's Hospital. Or we ask for food for the food bank. Think of something creative, people love it. And they love to give gifts.

There have been a couple of times when an organization wasn't able to pay Mike or I for our speaking engagement. We asked if it was possible to donate a book to the library. It was amazing, but the answer was usually yes! There was a genealogy association that wouldn't pay speakers but was happy to add a book in the genealogical section of the library. The nameplate inside the books notes their organization and my name. Perhaps a contribution of a new book to the library instead of a gift to a family member or co-worker might be appropriate!

The Queen of England has a particular problem that we don't have. Whenever she receives a gift, the date and who gave the gift is noted. Then, when that person visits her, the gift is brought out of storage and displayed. It is important to know what kind of occasion, because there are state and personal occasions. Gifts received for personal occasions can be kept personally, but gifts received from state occasions would be passed along to the next person holding that job title (the Queen/King of England, the Prince of Wales, etc.).

Gift Giving

Does Madison Avenue rule your life? Does the dollar rule? There are other gifts that take a little more creativity than just buying a present and wrapping it up.

For many families, they provide a *wish list* of the items for Christmas. This is very practical.

If the list system doesn't appeal to you, start thinking *smaller is better,* or considers subscriptions to magazines (that can be renewed on a yearly basis). What magazine would a friend like but wouldn't buy for themselves. I gave my Aunt Frances a subscription to *Majesty Magazine,* after I found out that she also enjoyed reading about the Royals but the price of the magazine was out of her budget.

How about a AAA membership? What about a night at a hotel or bed and breakfast?

The Royal family starts shopping immediately after Christmas for gifts. Typically, while at a farmer's market or an arts and crafts engagement, they might pick up a little something for their siblings, aunts and uncles or parents. A little something is correct. One year, Princess Anne (the only daughter of Queen Elizabeth II) was delighted when she received a door mat for Christmas.

A gift idea that I like for a newly wed couple is to note what china pattern the couple selected for their wedding. Then at the wedding or in conversations after the wedding finding out if they received a complete china set. If not, then at Christmas, birthdays and anniversaries we added additional pieces to the set.

Gift Book

Ann Gambrell, a professional organizer from Torrance California had this tip when I attended her seminar: buy and carry a small hardcover notebook (one that you find at a drug store on sale for less than a dollar with a hard cover). On each page, list the individuals that you are buying Christmas presents for. Retain this book year after year. We don't remember, but they do!

Gifts—Re-cycling

Some families give a white elephant gift. Instead of getting something brand new, they give an item that they already have. These can be great fun and hilarious entertainment. My cousin Curt and I passed along a blue yarn doll to each other for years. Usually there was something in the yarn doll. It was fun! Another friend and I would send each other Dick and Jane cards.

Another family has a treasure hunt. Inside a box under the Christmas tree is a wrapped gift. When the gift is opened, there is a clue (map, poem, riddle, instructions) to the next location. There are several locations and at the last spot is the present.

There is a game where each person receives a number through the number of people participating. Each person has brought and wrapped a gift, which is placed in the center of the room.

The person with #1 selects any gift from the center and unwraps it. The person with #2 can take the gift from #1 **or** select a gift from the center. If #2 takes #1 gift's, #1 then chooses from the center and unwraps it.

The person with #3 can take a gift from #1 or #2 or can select a gift from the middle. If a gift is taken from a person, that person selects from the center. This procedure is followed until the very last person. After the last person, #1 can then *take* a gift from anyone.

Kids and Gifts

With as much advertising that is done on Saturday morning television, it is sometime a wonder how we grew up with out all these new toys. But we did.

A couple of suggestions for helping the children prepare for Christmas and their toys.

First, at some point before Christmas (maybe December 1st) have the kids go through their closets, toy boxes, the living room, the dining room, the den and the storage area and take a look at the toys that they have.

Have them give to charity those toys that they have out grown or don't have all the parts. Then take the toys and the child down to the organization so that they can see how much happiness their gifts bring others.

Establish one in—one out rule for toys. If you know how many toys you will be giving then you can select the number. Or on Christmas morning (or whenever the presents are opened) after the gifts are opened, then the children choose what toys they want to donate.

Traditions

Holiday traditions are important to us, but what are they? Have you sat down to think about what holiday traditions are important to you and your family? Why do you do it?

When I was growing up, Santa Claus would bring our Christmas tree and stick it in the snow. It never occurred to me that this wasn't traditional with other families.

Most of the time, traditions are developed because they meet a need. What need does the tradition that you follow meet. Is it necessary to follow tradition (or the activity) each year? Would it be possible to skip a year? My father gave my mother a holiday plant (Easter lily or Poinsettia). I wish that my husband, Mike would learn that tradition!

Music

Do you have special holiday music? Where do you file (or store) this collection? Do you store it with the holiday decorations or do you store it with the other music? If you are storing it with the other music, all year long you will have to *walk over it* to get to the favorites. On the other hand, it the holiday music is stored with the holiday ornaments, then you can't listen to the holiday music until you get out the holiday ornaments!

The rule in our house is that holiday music can't be played until the day after Halloween! Around the first part of October (and in some years, the middle of September) the stores are starting to put out their holiday ornaments. I get excited about playing Christmas songs, but I have to wait. However, I do have over 40 cassette tapes and it does take about two months to play all of the tapes. By January 15, I am so tired of this stuff, I'd like to skip a Christmas. But about August/September, I am getting excited about Christmas all over again!

To solve both problems about where to store the holiday music (with the other tapes or with the decorations) we dedicate a separate box for the music. The music is stored with the ornaments but it is the last thing to be put away (which means that it is very easy to get to but without pulling out all the decorations). Sometimes, I will store the tapes in my closet so that I have easy access to them.

Also, Mike and I have Santa hats that are fun to wear while we start decorating the house. These hats, like the music, are one of the last things put away so that we can enjoy playing Santa while decorating.

Ornaments

More than any thing else, the memories and historical significance of Christmas are found in the Christmas ornaments. In addition to the enjoyment of the Christmas ornaments, do you have any further plans for the ornaments (such as passing them onto your children)?

If so, have you left a legacy of who, what, where, when and how? Who purchased the ornament, where did you get it, when did you get it, who would you like to give the ornament to?

How are you storing the ornaments? Wherever you store them, remember that consideration is taken for moisture, heat and bugs. Plastic containers (Rubbermaid products) are a good alternative.

If you have a *stable* location for storing the ornaments, how are you packing the ornaments? Do you individually wrap each ornament? Would it be faster and more efficient to just place the ornaments in their box without the wrapping? Egg cartons are great to use for small ornaments.

Typically, when Mike and I are traveling, I like to pick up a Christmas ornament from the area to remember the trip. When we were in Buenos Aries, Argentina, we found a cute Christmas shop. I picked up three or four items that were unusual. Back in the hotel room, I took a closer look at the items and they were from Ohio USA!

Planning For Next Year

After the holidays are over, I use the time to sit down and write a letter to myself. I put this in the file folder/three-ring notebook and look it over about August. In the speaking business, August slows down and I try to get as much done as I can to prepare for the holidays.

What things would I have liked to do but ran out of time?

What went well this year that I would like to do again? What would you like to do next year?

What didn't go the way I planned and why?

When shopping for Christmas, when possible, shop during the off hours. Make of list of what (or who) you'll be shopping for—don't deviate! Take with you cloth (grocery) bags so that you can put your purchases into the cloth bag which is easier to carry and they don't break or rip!!

Take out the extras from your purse or wallet. Take along only those essential things. Don't take your library card, all credit cards, pictures of the family and the next door neighbors. If you lose your wallet, there are only a couple of things that need to be reported and replaced.

Do you feel sad the day after Christmas and there are no presents under the tree? Wrap a couple of empty boxes. They are the first presents under the tree and are still there after Christmas day.

Lights

Have you ever tested the Christmas tree lights before putting them away only to find that the next Christmas just before putting the lights on the tree you check them one more time only to find that there is one or more bulbs that are burnt out? I could never figure out this phenomenon.

Store the string of lights in a zip-lock bag. The reason the light bulbs would burn out without ever being used has something to do with being exposed to the air. By creating an airless environment, you are extending the life of the bulbs.

The Royals do a lot of their Christmas shopping by catalogs. Or they might go to the local department store first thing in the morning when it's not crowded (alright, before it's open—but it's still not crowded).

365 Ways To Prepare For Christmas
by David E. Monn
Price: $5.99 Paperback 277 pages
ISBN: 0061093300

76 Ways To Get Organized For Christmas
by Bonnie McCullough and Bev Cooper
Price: $3.99 Paperback 118 pages Revised
ISBN: 0312929404

Checklist For A Perfect Christmas
by Judith Blahnik
Price: $6.99
ISBN: 0385482213

Christmas Is Coming
by Emilie Barnes
Price: $16.99
ISBN: 1565079124
This Christmas planner is filled with calendars, gifts and card charts, party plans, and helpful lists.

Chapter 9—Clutter Bug's Keys to Success

1. Invite other over to help you decorate.

2. Set the table with the good china as a decoration—like they do in department stores.

3. Give gifts that don't create clutter.

4. Start planning for next year the day after.

5. Put lights in zip-lock bags. 

Clutterology

GETTING RID OF CLUTTER AND GETTING ORGANIZED!

CHAPTER 10

What Can I Do to Make It:

Simpler? (reduce the number)

1. ____________________

2. ____________________

3. ____________________

Cleaner? (wipe it off)

1. ____________________

2. ____________________

3. ____________________

Neater? (close drawers, close cabinets)

1. ____________________

2. ____________________

3. ____________________

More organized?

1. ____________________

2. ____________________

3. ____________________

What area can you go to work on immediately?

1. ____________________

You Can Run But You Can't Hide!

Now it's time to get started. Pick a location, any location. Start out small. Get four containers and start at the door. Work clockwise around the room.

1. **Route it.** These are the items that don't belong in this room.

2. **Do it.** These are items that need to be taken care of or fixed. Do you find yourself saying "I wish this would _______ (close easier, be taller, move faster, move slower, etc.)" These are exactly the types of comments that will help you to **change your environment** to meet your needs. The first few times these unconscious, under-the-breath, comments may not register with your mind, but try to catch these moments.

3. **Give it away.** These are items that you would like to give away. Use large, very strong trash bags instead of a box. Bags accommodate different (odd) sizes. Once the decision has been made, you can't see inside the bag.

4. **Toss it.** These will go in the trash. Use a trash bag so once the item is tossed, you don't see it again (and start missing it).

Keeper or Memory Box

In the olden days, when an unmarried girl started to prepare for married life, she would have a hope chest. The hope chest would include clothes, baby outfits that she made, a quilt, dishes, etc.

Nowadays, a hope chest doesn't have the purpose it once did, but they are still wonderful locations to collect hopes and dreams.

My father gave each one of the children (some of us were older than others by the time he got around to it) a re-finished trunk. He would buy the trunk at auctions (or perhaps he found them at the dump). He would bring them home, replace all the hardware on the outside, fix up the inside and finish off the exterior. My trunk moved with me many, many times.

What that trunk became was a place to store all the papers and objects that I wanted to keep. I remember for a long time that there was a paper mache' orange piñata in there that I made for a Girl Scout badge.

If I wanted to save something but there wasn't enough room in the trunk. The idea is that I could pick and choose what items to keep and what items to toss.

If you are planning to store any special clothing (wedding dress, baptismal gown), lay it in acid-free tissue (which can be purchased at art supply stores). Then wrap in washed cotton to avoid sharp creases (which can weaken the fabric). Take out and refold every year to further prevent creasing. If you see signs of mold or discoloring, then the fabric has not been able to breathe.

If you don't have a father that is so handy, it is possible to buy trunks, chests, footlockers or banker boxes for this purpose. Use a box for grades 1-6. Then during the 7th grade year, reduce the items for grades 1-6 down to a box or two. Continue this system through 6-12. Then in 12th grade, go through all the boxes, saving just the precious few.

Lillian Vernon has a 6-drawer school chest stand-alone unit for this type of system.

If there are things that are difficult to part with, change the media. Take a picture of it, clip a corner off the fabric, videotape it or scan it so that it can be viewed on the computer.

Also, ask yourself why do you want to remember? What if you didn't remember, would that alter your life? Are you documenting an event such as the first day of school? Who would care other than you? Take steps so that person (or those individuals) have access or know about your desire to share this information with them.

Murphy's Hope Chest Factory
283 Derby Street
Salem MA 01972
800-464-0252

Annual Event

Set a time to de-clutter (spring, New Year's Eve, your birthday or a holiday). This is your date to go through all the closets and in general de-clutter your environment.

I know of one lady that uses the month of her birthday to do her yearly maintenance (doctor, dentist, and eyes). That way, she never has to remember.

Touch everything. It is amazing how things become a part of the structure. Touching it will trigger the mind that this might be clutter. (See page 104.)

Hire (Get) Help

Sometimes, it will help by getting outside help. Sometimes a friend can help. Help comes in all different sizes and shapes.

If you have a computer, there are some grocery stores that will deliver, saving you time. What do you buy that is the same all the time? Perfume, underwear, shoes?

Hire someone to come in and clean the house—monthly, quarterly, yearly or whenever you feel it is necessary. An extra pair of hands and you working along with them will speed up the process.

For many years, with roommates, we had a professional cleaning crew come in to clean (once a month). They became the standard we worked with. If one roommate was messier than another, most of the time waiting a month was do-able. Also, once something is clean, it is easier to keep it clean so picking up becomes simple.

When I got married and having several home-based businesses to run, there were always other projects to handle rather than cleaning the house. It takes two people working four hours to complete the task every other week. That is eight hours of work, time I don't have.

Ask your dry cleaners if they deliver. There are more cleaners that are delivering which is a time saver.

Hire a high school student to come in and assist you. They have a tremendous amount of energy for a short period of time.

Whether it is a plumber, painter or just an extra pair of hands, get help. Mike's degree is in electrical engineering. It is faster (and usually cheaper) if I hire someone to come in and fix it. It never fails that even with a professional there is always an unforeseen problem that occurs. If Mike was working on the project, he would get mad and upset. Often times although I think the cost would be expensive, usually in the long run, it is very cost effective.

Sometimes it is helpful to have a trusted friend that can help you out. The old saying *two heads are better than one* in this case could be revised to two sets of hands are better than one set. Also, just by asking the buddy "should I keep this?" becomes an easy answer for them where it is a difficult answer for us.

I rely on my husband's advise when it comes to clothes that I'm wearing. I have a tendency to wear clothes past their prime. So when he says "Nancy I think it's time to give that to Goodwill" no matter how much I want to say but ..., I don't.

Sometimes getting professional help is necessary. If you contact the national office or access the web site you can find the professional organizer closest to you. The association of professional organizers is:

National Association of Professional Organizers (NAPO)
1033 La Posada Drive, Suite 220
Austin TX 78752-3880
512-454-8626 or 512-454-3036 fax www.napo.net

Messies Anonymous
5025 SW 114th Avenue
Miami FL 33165
305-271-8404
For a list of self-help groups and information about starting your own self-help group, contact Messies Anonymous. To receive a sample of the newsletter, send a self-addressed stamped envelope.

Pretend To ...

Sometimes, we have to trick ourselves or play games with ourselves. By pretending that what we are about to do isn't sooo serious or a life and death situation, we actually can make the change. If it doesn't work it's OK to go back to what we were doing before. Here are some suggestions for pretending:

1. Pretend to go paperless in your office (if you have a computer). What if you had to go paperless, what would your office look like? Would the address or card file be put on the computer? Are there papers in the file cabinet that could be scanned onto the computer? Can your computer be used as a fax? What would you do? Implement one great idea!!

2. Pretend that you have to move tomorrow. Pack up all the things that you don't need right now and put them in a box. See what comes back out of the box that you do need.

3. Pretend that you are snow bound for a month. What meals can you fix without buying another morsel? What clothes could you use instead of going shopping? What games could the kids invent for themselves?

4. Pretend that your house was flooded. What items would make you cry or your heartbreak if you saw them soaked with water? What steps can you take to save those items?

5. Pretend that you won the lottery and now, can start over. What would you give up?

6. Pretend that an earthquake (or fire) destroyed your home, what two or three items were you able to protect?

7. Pretend that you are going camping (or traveling) and what you bring along you have to carry yourself. What would you **not** bring along?

8. Pretend that your kids or family don't want the things that you have been keeping for them, what would you do with them now?

Change the Lightbulbs

One of the most underestimated benefits is to change the light bulbs. Either replace them to a higher wattage or change the type of light fixture or install better fixtures. There is the psychological benefit from better lighting. It's also cheaper and faster than painting.

Too Convenient

Now, this might sound a little weird, which is why I am putting this advice in the last chapter. Have you placed things a little too conveniently or over organized just a bit too much?

Are the chocolates that are sitting on top of your desk getting consumed quickly by you and others because they're out? Have you provided a little too much entertainment for the family in the bathroom, which would turn a quick job on their parts into a several minute project? Are all your spices in alphabetical order and you found that you are going back to re-alphabetize them?

Sometimes what we try the first time, although our intentions are good, just doesn't work. Don't let that discourage you. Trial and error is a wonderful teacher, but more importantly than that, is sometimes we need to learn from our own experiences. My telling you, your mother telling you, or even your spuse telling you, won't get the point across, we need to try it ourselves.

Vacuum Cleaner

Your vacuum cleaner could use a yearly tune up. Look in the yellow pages for a local service store and take it in for service. Usually, the cost isn't that expensive.

Setting Clocks/Watches Ahead

It has been suggested that by setting clocks ahead 5-10 minutes that this will give you those few extra minutes if you're running late.

My mother had this idea, so all of the clocks in the house were five minutes fast. But, it didn't work. We all knew the clocks were five minutes fast, so we just adjusted our timing by five minutes.

If this technique is going to work, then you can't know how fast clock is. I use this method in the bedroom and in my bathroom. The first thing in the morning, when I am not thinking clearly, I see the time and I start moving faster. But, I randomly add a few minutes to the clock. Sometimes it's two minutes fast, sometimes it's twenty minutes fast.

The clock at Sandringham, England (the Royal family country home) were set ahead one hour for years (by Edward VII and George V). The reason was so that the gentlemen could get in an extra hour of hunting.

Daylight savings time is an attempt to give us more daylight hours in a day.

Shopping At Discount Stores

A very wise friend of ours has a rule not to shop at a certain discount store. Not because the prices aren't great, but it seems that every time he buys something, the *some assembly required* project is missing parts or something or another happens. It takes three trips to the store to get the project completed.

Do you have a store like that in your neighborhood? They don't seem to get it right the first time. Our tailor is an example, he never meets his due dates, so I frequently call before I travel to his shop. Add in all the costs of a product (see page 17).

Working With Others

Many times, I set up systems for our household and office. Because we are two people, Mike and I need to communicate. Since Mike frequently will carry things up and down the stairs for me so that I have both hands free to operate my crutches, we developed a system for what is needed to go to certain places.

Items on the left-hand side of the steps would go all the way down to the garage and items on the right-hand side of the steps would go to the next floor down (the living room, dining room, and kitchen area). On each floor, there is another staging area where he places the items and then I get around to putting them where they belong.

Well, each time Mike was about to pick up the items off the floor to carry down, he would yell at me, "Where do these go?" It might have been three hours ago that I put them there or there might be 25 small things for him to carry down. Each time, I would tell him.

One day, Mike again yelled at me, "Where do these go?" and I snapped. "Don't you remember? The things on the right go downstairs and the things on the left go to the garage?" Mike replied "No, I don't remember." Well, suddenly it become very clear. Although **we** had set up the system and agreed on it, and although Mike proudly boasts about his great memory, this was one thing he didn't remember. I don't know why I said it, but then I snapped, "What do I have to do to help you remember?" "Label it!" What an easy solution that was.

When it comes to working with other people, whether they are co-workers or family members, forcing your ideas or standards on them may work for a short period of time or it might not work at all.

The best suggestion is to set an example. Create opportunities to develop systems together that work for both. In the above example, we had talked about it and had decided. He forgot. It happens. Mike wasn't forgetting deliberately or maliciously; he was just being Mike. The key was what would it take to help him to remember? There were all kinds of answers (put a sticky note on each item, do it myself, or even keep answering his question each time).

People aren't going to change until they are ready or until they want to. Try to create conflict, no not the kind where you are fighting but the kind that is slightly uncomfortable.

I wanted to help Mike with his files but until he found a need for a better system, I just stayed out of his way and waited for his system to crash. Then he was open to alternative options.

Why Organization Might Not Work

There are times when no matter what you do, the **system** just doesn't work.

In an office environment, co-workers, supervisors, or bosses may not *get with the program*. There are several reasons why.

Perhaps the individual likes having people wait on them. Gordy, where is the report for the Jones meeting? Consciously or unconsciously this type of individual feels that part of their power is in controlling people and things.

Perhaps the individual needs to be needed. There is great satisfaction when a child asked mom "where are my tennis shoes?" There is a pleasure to helping and serving people. Little does the individual know that in the long run they aren't helping each other—isn't this called co-dependency?

Perhaps the individual is just disorganized. Their systems work for them and they see no need or reason to change—especially if this person is your boss or a superior. This type of circumstance is difficult, however, a very strong team (boss/secretary, supervisor/assistant) where the secretary can help the boss and the boss can really really really trust the secretary.

Perhaps the individual believes in *just in case*. There is no logical reason for keeping certain items but no amount of logic will encourage this individual to get rid of the clutter. Oh well!

Remove the Temptations

Like anyone who is in recovery, sometimes our defenses over temptation aren't very strong. If need be, remove yourself from these temptations.

If you love to shop by mail order, remove your name from their mailing lists. What you don't see, you won't miss.

If you love to go to the mall to shop, limit the times that you go to the mall. Perhaps once a month, or once a quarter, or once a year, or as a reward for completion of a project.

If trade shows are a necessary part of your job, limit the number of trade shows that you attend per year.

Ransom Box

This is a great idea for people with children (or people that act like children).

Announce that starting today (or a couple days from now) that any items left in the common areas (areas that everyone uses) by 5:00 p.m. (some convenient time) will be picked up by you (or the ransom police or any fictitious character). Individuals can buy items out of the ransom box (daily or weekly).

I have heard of a similar use of a ransom box where a box (or location) all the *lost* items would be stored. For instance, the kids have gone to school and you are picking up the house but the kids have left their baseball mitts in the living room. Instead of putting them back where they belong, they just go in the box (in that room or on that floor, etc.). You're not picking up after the kids but the house is picked up to your level of satisfaction.

Quick Start

An ideal situation would be to be able to handle a piece of paper only once. Realistically, that is not very practical. However, there are times when I deliberately handle the papers only once. There are times when I am constantly putting several papers aside without dealing with them. This is a **game** that I play with myself to get that stuff handled. This even means that if I have to pick up a document and walk clear across the room to take care of it, I will do it!

An average time for a person to organize a house is between 6 and 12 weeks. However, not many people are average. Keep at it for however long it takes you. The present condition of the house or office happened over years so the progress that you make is actually much faster.

There will be times when nothing seems to get done. Then all of a sudden, chunks, projects, activities, and things just fall into place. It's like working on a jigsaw puzzle. It seems no progress is made, then all of a sudden every piece that you pick up fits!

You may wish to start with the big (size) projects that are easy (degree of difficulty) to do first. You see those projects when you walk into a room (making the bed) instead of small projects that are difficult (organizing the photo albums).

Start on something while you are waiting—for the microwave or during television commercials. Many times we are already doing something while waiting for the microwave, but perhaps open a drawer and clean it out real fast.

Although we don't watch much real time television, I love the commercials. I have 30-60 seconds to get something done. This helps me in three ways. First it gets me off the sofa doing something (this is call exercise). Secondly it accomplishes a task and third it makes me hurry to do it—I don't have all day. Surprisingly, I get a number of things done. If the program isn't holding my attention, my eyes drift around the room and I start planning my next mad dash.

Emotions

When I moved from Minnesota to California, I remember calling my mother in tears and feeling homesick those first few months. Instead of giving any sympathy, Mom said "Isn't that great!" What a surprise! Then she went on to say that in order to be homesick, I had to have something that I liked/loved and now missed. Wow, what wonderful words. My mother's wisdom became infinitely wiser the more miles were between us.

When it comes time to toss out or get rid of some of the things that have become friends or a part of our family, there may be a *pang* of feelings. Enjoy the feelings. They are a part of us.

Then in days, weeks, months or even years later, when you happen to recall that item, enjoy the homesickness. Wasn't it great to have something that you like to have feelings for?

Empty Space

Don't look at empty drawers or vacant walls as a negative. In fact, think of negative space as positive. There is an energy that is created when you open a drawer and it is possible to see everything in the drawer. It's not over crowded, it's not difficult to open or close, it's wonderful.

What's The Difference Between

When you are trying to decide whether to keep something or not, here are a few more questions to ask yourself. If things stay the same, there is no change!

- Keeping it and not being able to find it when you need it.
- Not keeping it?

- Clipping coupons and not using them?
- Clipping coupons and buying products you wouldn't otherwise by?
- Shopping for the lowest price per unit value?

- Keeping a souvenirs and never looking at it?
- Tossing it?

- Having a pile of unread reading material and thinking *there might be something important or informative in this?*
- Tossing the unread material?

- Having clothes in your closet that you can't wear?

- Having clothes in your closet that you can wear?

- Buying something expensive but it doesn't work for you?
- Tossing it?

- Videotaping programs off the television and not watching them?
- Starting clean (over)?

I don't have the answers to these questions—only you do!

Change Your Environment

Throughout this book I have been saying to change your environment rather than to change you. The paradox is that by changing your environment after a while, the environment will change you.

As I have stated previously (see page 162) when I was just out of college, I started to use a cleaning crew. Because I know that they are coming in to clean, I can pick up. It is a whole lot easier to pick up than clean up. The surprising part is that I now pick up quicker and faster than before. The environment has changed me.

Chapter 10—Clutter Bug's Keys to Success

1. Reduce. Get rid of as much stuff as possible.

2. Simplify. If at all possible, simply your life.

3. This is a life-long process. Some years life will be easy. Other years, getting through the year is an achievement.

4. Use determines storage. Those things that are used on a daily basis are kept closest to your body. Those not used on a regular basis are stored.

8

A

B

C

D

E

F

G

H

T

U

V

W

X

Y

We'd love to hear from you. Let us know your reactions, and the things you did or didn't like about this book. If you need more forms or would like to keep the book intact, make a photocopy of this page. Send us photos of a before and after.

- How you've made use of the information.
- What actually worked for you?
- What other suggestions do you have for us?

Thanks for your help.

Comments: ____

____

____

____

____

____

Your Name:____

Address:____

❑ Would you like to subscribe to the Clutter Bug Newsletter?

❑ You have my permission to quote from my comments, and use these quotations in ads, brochures, mail, and other promotions used to market the book.

Signed:_______________________________ Date:__________

Clutterology
6318 W Ridgepath CtRancho Palos Verdes, CA 90275-3248
www.RoundsMiller.com